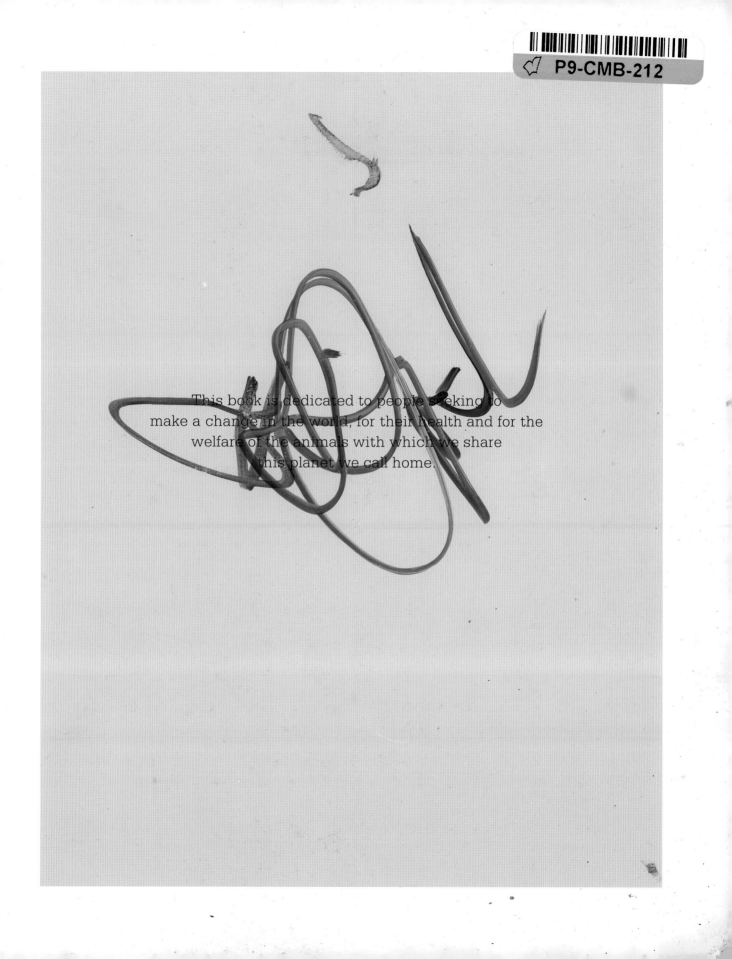

This book is dedicated to people seeking to make a change in the world, for their health and for the welfare of the animals with which we share this planet we call home.

Contents

Introduction

Veegun? Vaygun? Veggan? Nope. It's "vegan," and let us tell you what it means to us.

Two separate roads can lead to veganism. Some people eat a plant-based diet and refrain from eating animals for the health benefits; other people do it because of their compassion for animals. Some do it for both reasons. And although both types of people technically fall into the same category—vegan—they don't always see eye to eye. Sometimes there can be a cavernous divide between these two groups, but we're here to welcome them all and to win the battle for both our health *and* for the animals.

In the following paragraphs, you'll read how Gerrie came to veganism for her health and how Joni became vegan for the animals. We're here to show you how the two really do overlap in so many ways, and that there is a whole lot that we can learn from each other. It's really exciting.

This book is for anyone looking to make a switch to a plant-based diet, either for your health, for the animals, or for both! Regardless of your reason, we want to provide recipes that everyone can enjoy. There's a lot of information and opinions out there about which foods are "healthy." There are also a lot of edicts, such as don't consume too much oil, cut out oils altogether, and/or cut out salts. But we know that going vegan can be challenging enough, so if we then also told you to cut out sugar, salt, or oil, you might find the whole process too hard and just give up. That's not what we want to happen! So we'll include some transitional foods—such as vegan mayo, vegan cheese, and vegan meat—along with some really healthy, tasty, vegetable-heavy recipes for those of you looking to cure whatever ails you with food.

We want to show even the biggest skeptics that a melty, gooey grilled cheese sandwich can still be made without the use of animal products, and how you can make simple swaps at the supermarket for vegan versions of traditionally non-vegan items.

The interesting thing is that, even in some of the no-added-sugar-oil-salt recipes, we still rely heavily on naturally occurring fats, sugars, and salts, so the overall calorie and fat counts tend to be similar, even though neither of us counts calories or emphasizes counting calories. The recipes with no added oils, sugar, or salt are simply much healthier, and the nutrient density per calorie is much higher.

When you eat a well-thought-out, plant-based diet, the need for calorie counting is almost eradicated. So there will be no calorie counts listed for our recipes. We also don't believe in fixating on the amount of carbs, fats, and proteins, so you won't see any references to these macronutrients either. The focus of eating well should be on eating wholesome foods that are nutrient dense. The beauty of these types of foods is that they are naturally low in calories, and they provide fats, carbs, and proteins in a natural, wholesome way. We will give you suggestions for replacing sugar, salt, and added fats, when warranted, but this book is not a weight-loss book, because *losing weight and becoming healthy do not always equate.*

WellBeings

While working together on this book, we began looking for a word that would encompass all that we love. We love the animals, we love the planet, we love each other, and we love ourselves.

The word vegan is very specific in its meaning. According to *Webster's*, a vegan is a strict vegetarian who does not eat animal products. Okay, fine, that's true, but it doesn't tell the whole story. It doesn't convey the compassion that lives within us.

In our search, we came up with all sorts of silly terms, but when we read the meaning of the term well-being, we knew we were on to something. Once again referring to our friend *Webster's*, well-being is defined as being healthy, happy, or prosperous.

So we have decided to call ourselves *WellBeings* (WeBes for short!) instead of vegans because, while all WellBeings are indeed vegan, all vegans are not necessarily WellBeings. We invite you all to join us.

Each one of us has our reasons for making the choice to live a compassionate and less-cruel life. Whether for our health, or the health of the animals, we all have a story to tell on how we came to be WellBeings. Here are ours.

Gerrie's Story

I had the good fortune of growing up in a traditional middle class family with a breadwinning father and a very dutiful and dedicated stay-at-home mom. We were a typical American family with a very typical American diet. My mother thought she was being a "good" mother by serving us what she had been taught was a "well-balanced" diet. In fact, I distinctly remember not being allowed to leave the table until I had tried a little of everything and I had eaten all of my vegetables. However, if I had known then what I know now, the food on my plate would have been a lot different. I would probably still have all of my organs. I would have been able to have children. And I would not have lost my mother to cancer at the early age of forty-five.

Even though I was fed what was thought of as a "healthy" diet, I grew up not being a very healthy person. As a child, I could count on having tonsillitis or strep throat at least once a year, plus numerous colds. I was always told that my illnesses were due to the bad sinuses that ran in our family. All through my teenage years, I struggled with my weight, and I suffered tremendous cramps, water weight gain, and mood swings with my "monthly visitor." In my junior year of high school, my appendix became severely infected and ruptured before the doctors detected the problem. I came closer to dying than I would have liked.

When I was twenty-five years old, my gallbladder had to be removed due to "gallstones too numerous to count." In fact, it took the doctors three months to diagnose my condition because gallstones were unheard of in a twenty-five-year-old in great physical shape. As if all of these health problems were not enough, I developed endometriosis in my early thirties, and by age thirty-five, I had my right ovary and fallopian tube removed. I was fortunate enough to have a wonderful fertility doctor who was able to save my left ovary and fallopian tube so that I could continue to try to become pregnant. However, after many years of trying, I was still never able to have children. Exhaustive testing never uncovered the reason why.

At the age of forty, I decided that I didn't want to undergo any more major surgeries. I was running out of organs to have removed and still have my body function normally! At this point in my life, I decided to start researching on how I could make positive changes to my physical health.

I became a voracious reader, combing through every book on nutrition and diet I could find. Then one day on TV, I heard actress Marilu Henner being interviewed and talking about her new book, *The Total Health Makeover*. After ten years of studying anatomy, physiology, Eastern and Western medicine, macrobiotics, vegetarianism, acupuncture, and chiropractics, and experimenting with different eating behaviors, Marilu had come up with a lifestyle that afforded her optimum health and vitality. In fact, she looked so good and had so much energy that her friends, family, and fellow actors all wanted to know what she was doing. After much encouragement, she decided to share her program in a book. I was intrigued by the information she gave in her TV interview, and I went right out and purchased the book.

In short, Marilu's book changed my health—and my life. I took two years to incorporate all of Marilu's recommended dietary changes by doing one step at a time, and I only progressed to the next step when I had mastered the current one. With each step, my health improved. After I gave up dairy foods, the weekly, painful sinus headaches I had experienced for years disappeared. When I eliminated red meat from my diet and added in more whole grains, leafy greens, and vegetables, my chronic constipation disappeared. As welcome and incredible as all of those improvements were, my biggest life-changing moment came once I had completed all of the recommended steps.

Marilu had stated in her book that all of the problems women suffer during our monthly menstruation are due to our diets. In short, I did not believe it. I couldn't believe that the ten pounds of water weight gain, cramping, bloating, mood swings, and facial breakouts were caused by what I ate. It took me untold amounts of painkillers to get through the first two days of every menstrual cycle. After experiencing these same symptoms like clockwork every month for more than twenty years, two months to the day after I incorporated all of my new-found dietary changes, I started my period, and I didn't even know it! All of those symptoms were nonexistent. I became a believer for life. Marilu was right. Everything I had been experiencing really was a result of what I was eating!

I realized that if I hadn't believed that we "are what we eat," then I knew the majority of people didn't understand or believe it either. At that point, I decided to change my career and dedicate the rest of my life to studying nutrition and helping people become more aware of how their dietary choices affect their health—and also the health of the planet.

The next sixteen years were an amazing time of learning and validating that I had made the correct decision for a new career path. I went back to school and graduated at the age of fifty with a bachelor's of science degree in food science with emphasis in nutrition. Through my classes in anatomy, nutrition, and chemistry, I learned that our bodies are amazing healing machines, and my studies helped me understand why we "are what we eat." The next seven years of developing and selling an all-natural food product gave me an incredible insight into what really goes into processed food. I learned that manufacturers do not have to declare everything that is put into food products! But the most life-changing information came from my current employment. Over the past four years, working as a Healthy Eating Specialist for Whole Foods Market, I have had the amazing pleasure of studying with many doctors who have been preventing and reversing conditions—such as heart disease, cancer, high cholesterol, diabetes, digestive issues, and many autoimmune diseases—with food, not drugs. Through studying with incredible doctors such as Joel Fuhrman M.D. (author of *Eat for Life, Eat for Health, Super Immunity,* and *Ending Diabetes*), Colin Campbell, Ph.D. in nutrition, biochemistry, and microbiology (author of *The China Study* and *Worth*), Caldwell Esselstyn, M.D. (author of *Prevent and Reverse Heart Disease*), his son Rip Esselstyn (author of *Engine 2 Diet* and *My Beef with Meat*), John A. McDougall, M.D. (author of *Digestive Tune Up* and *The Starch Solution*), I have learned and experienced personally that food is for nourishment, and it is also a powerful healing tool.

After having access to the overwhelmingly amazing research and the results achieved by these doctors over the past forty years, I made the decision to adopt a completely plant-based diet. Since making this decision, I have enjoyed a level of health that I had never before experienced. In addition, over the past four years, I have helped numerous people adopt a plant-based diet. I watched as their heart disease, diabetes, and other conditions disappeared, and their lives were totally changed.

There's no doubt in my mind that a vegan (or 100 percent plant-based) diet is the most effective way to achieve and maintain optimum health. I intend to live, teach, and share this way of eating with all who want to learn—for the rest of my very long and healthy life!

Joni's Story

I am, first and foremost, an ethical vegan. The health benefits I have enjoyed through my veganism have simply been a bonus.

I grew up in a family where hunting and fishing were the norm, and stuffed animal heads on walls were common. My parents were divorced, and my amazing mom made sure that we had a hot meal together every single night. But between her full-time job and my and my sister's swim team and water polo practice, school, marching band (yes, I played the tuba in marching band!), and other extracurricular activities, there was little time left for home-cooked meals. Prepackaged convenience foods—such as boxed macaroni and cheese, hamburger meal mixes, and minute steaks made appearances almost every night.

I became a half-hearted vegetarian in high school when my favorite singer, my beloved, Morrissey, told me meat was "murder." A girlfriend and I did an oral report on the horrors of animal testing and vivisection. We even made a 'zine to pass out to the class, and we played the video for "Meat Is Murder" in the background while we gave our report. (My teacher was so impressed that she had us come back and do the report for two other classes that day.)

I'd always been anti-fur and against animal testing, but I faltered with my eating habits throughout early adulthood. I toyed with vegetarianism off and on, but I never fully committed.

As a swimmer and a water polo player in high school, I could shovel as much food into my mouth as I wanted and never had a weight problem. During the school year, I worked out for two hours, five nights a week, and I had meets and matches on the weekends. During the summer months, we had morning and evening practice for four hours each day!

Then I went to college. Although I was a dedicated swimmer, I wasn't very fast, and I only lasted one year on the team. I stopped the crazy workouts, but I kept up the crazy eating. It didn't take long for the pounds to pack on. I worked my way through school, so I relied heavily on cafeteria and fast food on my way to and from school and between classes. My "freshman fifteen" was more like "sophomore sixty."

Fast-forward a few more years. I was out of school and living with my soon-to-be husband. I had really begun to understand how bad fast food, processed foods, and all the other junk I was putting into my body was. I was extremely overweight and tired. It was time to get healthy.

I tried a lot of fad diets, and I lost and gained back a lot of weight over the next few years. In the back of my mind and deep in my heart, I knew what I needed to do.

In 2005, I decided to make it official and go vegan. I kicked it all off with a ten-day Master Cleanse on the 4th of July. I figured that if I could spend the entire holiday watching everyone else chow down on barbecue and guzzle soda and beer while I was only sipping on lemonade spiked with cayenne pepper, then I could do it for ten days. So I did. Then I changed to an almost completely raw diet until I married my husband in September 2005. I have been vegan ever since.

Once I was eating vegan, it became a lot more important to eat at home, because there were very few vegan restaurants at the time. I was cooking at home far more than I had ever done before. I learned about different cooking techniques from vegan cookbooks and websites. I began blogging about my adventures in the kitchen. I became obsessed. I bought vegan cookbooks left and right. I "veganized" old family favorite recipes, and I began to find my own voice in the vegan community. I began meeting up and doing outreach with other vegans.

At the same time, I started to learn about the horrors that were occurring on factory farms. I made a conscious effort to read all labels on my foods—and also on my body-care products and household chemicals. After all, going vegan wasn't only about what I was eating, but also about what I was wearing and about all of the products I was using in my life. I wanted my consumer dollars to support companies that were promoting animal-free products.

As time went on, I became more vocal with friends and family. I tried not to be preachy, but rather lead by example. Being vegan wasn't about what I *couldn't* eat, but more about all of the things I *could eat* without harming any living creature to have a tasty meal.

The more I have learned over the years, the more frustrated I get by the practices of factory farms, the industrialized food system, and the lies we are told by our own government about what is healthy. The fact that any amount of meat or dairy is recommended each day is simply a mystery to me.

I know it's tough to give up the foods we grew up loving. Almost every single day, I catch a whiff of barbecue or bacon, and my mouth waters. I can't help it. It's a physical response to my taste buds' "memories." But I don't waver in my veganism, because I know that it's wrong to eat the flesh of a sentient being.

Lucky for me—and you!— now is an awesome time to be vegan. So many products out there make it so easy to eat a plant-based diet. From chicken-less chicken, to cashew "cheese," to coconut ice cream, there really isn't any food we can't enjoy completely free of guilt. It's my goal to teach others how to live a compassionate and cruelty-free life. A life free of murder, torture, and exploitation. A life free of body shaming and name calling. A life free of animal products.

Let me end by saying that I'm in no way perfect. I don't grow my own food, and I admit to really enjoying some of the most ridiculous vegan convenience foods. But I'm a vegan in every sense of the word. I have a "V" tattooed below my right ear to remind me of it every single time I look into the mirror. (Yes, the tattoo ink is vegan!) This is a commitment I have made for life. I hope you'll find the courage to join me!

Our Goal

We wrote this book to share what we've learned on our journey and to guide you through yours. We would like to help you transition from a SAD/Sickness and Disease-promoting Diet to a HAPPY (Healthy and Planet-Preserving Yummy) one, while bridging the gap between the people looking to improve their health and those looking to improve the lives of the animals.

We hope you find this book enlightening, inspiring, and helpful on your journey to becoming a WellBeing.

Chapter 1

Do It for Your Health!

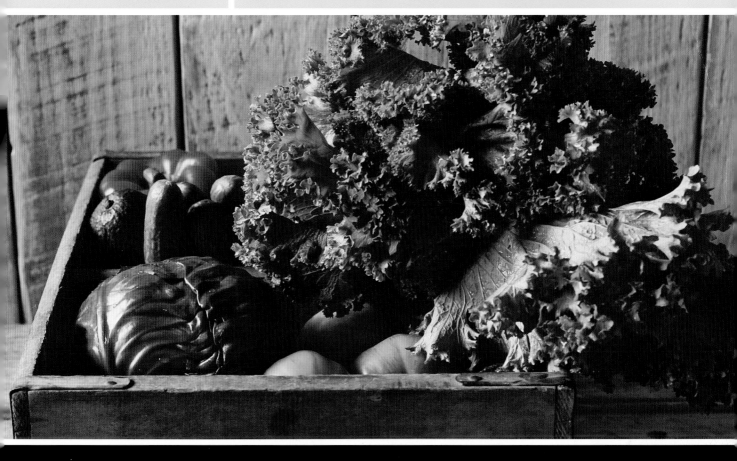

Whether you become a vegan for health, compassion, or both, everyone who eats should be educated about what's in our food and how our bodies use the food we eat.

In this chapter, we'll explore what is in the food we eat, how the food supply has changed over the past fifty years, and how that relates to the current state of our "WellBeing." You'll learn about an alkaline diet, why it is important for us to eat an alkaline diet, and how acidic foods affect digestion and the body's ability to absorb nutrients from our food. We will discuss the body's nutritional needs and what foods are the highest in those nutrients. We will also address some popular food myths out there.

Most important, we'll provide the steps you need to take to use your food as "medicine" to prevent and reverse many of the diseases and health conditions that are on the rise today.

What's in the Food We Eat?

For WeBes, understanding how our food is created is very important. We can't trust labels to tell us how food is produced. In fact, labels aren't even required to list all of the ingredients used in the product or the harmful chemicals used in the processing of ingredients that are listed on the labels. For example, manufacturers can use "processing aids" (e.g., chemicals that will help foods bake faster) and not declare them on the ingredient label. This is because the chemical should be gone once the product is done baking, and only a slight trace may be left. We should have the right to know that this chemical was added though. So, we need to do our own research. Lucky for you, we've already done a lot of the work. First, we'll start by taking a look at genetically modified foods, overprocessed foods, and "Frankenfoods."

GENETICALLY MODIFIED ORGANISMS

Essentially, a genetically modified organism (GMO) is an organism that is genetically altered at the DNA level. There is much controversy over GMO foods, and rightfully so because in order to create a GMO, genetic engineers most commonly use a bacteria or a virus in combination with an antibiotic as a vehicle to splice in a gene from another organism. As the laws exist right now, no regulations require companies to disclose if their foods are made using GMOs.

Most conventionally grown (non-organic) corn, soy, and sugar beet crops are genetically modified. In fact, according to the International Service for the Acquisition of Agri-biotech Applications (ISAAA) the area of land devoted to genetically modified crops has ballooned by 100 times since farmers first started growing the crops commercially in 1996. Over the past 17 years, millions of farmers in 28 countries have planted and replanted GMO crop seeds on a cumulative 3.7 billion acres of land.

For wheat in particular, chemical companies have introduced herbicide-ready crops to the market, then pulled them, then reintroduced them, and pulled them again, when the international market rejected them. Unfortunately, once GMOs are introduced into the food supply, it is hard to eliminate them. Over the years, random wheat crops have been tested and shown to be GMO crops.

What are the problems created through genetic engineering of food and crops? Genetic engineers continually encounter unintended side effects. For example, GM plants create toxins, react to weather differently, contain too many or too few nutrients, become diseased or malfunction, and die. When foreign genes are inserted, dormant genes may be activated or the functioning of genes may be altered, creating new or unknown proteins, or increasing or decreasing the output of existing proteins inside the plant. The effects of consuming these new combinations of proteins are unknown.

Scientists also experiment with inter-species genetic modification (transgenic). This is a real and present danger, both ethically and physically. It's now possible for plants to be engineered with genes taken from bacteria, viruses, insects, animals, or even humans. To name a few frightening combinations: Arctic fish genes gave tomatoes and strawberries tolerance to frost. Lightning bugs crossed with potatoes make them glow in the dark when they need watering. Human genes inserted into corn produced spermicide. Other trials have inserted jellyfish genes into corn, rice engineered with human genes, and corn engineered with hepatitis virus genes, just to name a few.

While this may all be in the name of science, we feel that we have a right to know what's in our food, especially if it involves inserting potentially dangerous allergens or animal products into our tomatoes!

It's interesting to consider that the time frame when GMOs became more prevalent is the same time frame that gluten, peanut, and soy allergies also began to climb exponentially.

OVERPROCESSED FOODS

What's the difference between picking an apple off a tree and opening a jar of store-bought apple-flavored "fruit strips"? The fruit strips are dramatically processed. The overprocessing, overpasteurization, and overuse of chemical additives and preservatives have also changed the makeup of our food. This makes it more difficult to digest properly and causes adverse reactions and allergies to what should be healthy, nutritious foods.

To make matters worse, highly processed foods contain very few, if any nutrients. They are also loaded with sugars, unhealthy fats, and sodium, all of which cause diseases such as diabetes, heart disease, and high blood pressure, just to name a few.

We also mentioned pasteurization. It's true that pasteurization creates a product that is free of harmful bacteria, which is something we all want. Yet there is really no reason to consume these often highly processed foods that do not provide nourishment. Cow, sheep, and goat milk, cheese, yogurt, and other dairy foods can simply be replaced with nondairy, plant-based versions. The high temperatures used to pasteurize fruit juices kill important health-promoting enzymes, making a good case to replace them with fresh squeezed and pressed juices.

So many foods today are also chock-full of chemical additives and preservatives. Our bodies are not equipped to digest and effectively eliminate preservatives and manmade chemicals in our food. Once these types of products are ingested, anything the body cannot eliminate or break down gets stored in fat. These substances then cause irritation and contamination to the body, resulting in disease. Many well-documented studies show a link between artificial preservatives and chemical additives and cancers and other diseases.

FRANKENFOODS

In 1950, the average chicken raised for meat weighed about 2 pounds (908 g). That's less than half of the average poultry chicken today. The breasts (the most desirable portion of the chicken) are so large on today's factory-farmed chickens that their legs cannot support their weight. How do these chickens grow so big? With the use of antibiotics, growth hormones, and selective breeding. The steriods cause the chickens to grow to the size of a six-month-old in only three months.

When our grandparents grew up, they most likely got their eggs from the same chicken that was slaughtered for Sunday dinner. Back then, most chickens and eggs came from small family farms. Technological advances—such as the discovery of vitamin D supplementation that allows chickens to be kept year-round without fear of ailments due to lack of sunlight—led to larger operations. Poultry farms grew bigger and bigger, eventually leading to the factory farms we see today.

Cows are raised similarly. Just like chickens, the dairy cows and beef cattle raised today are nothing like "Bessie" that Ma and Pa had to milk every morning on the family farm.

Large factory farms are not without problems. Housing many animals in a small space provides the perfect breeding ground for parasites, bacteria, and viruses. To try to combat this, even more antibiotics are fed to the animals.

In recent years, the amount of antibiotics being sold (over 30 million pounds, or 13,608 metric tons, in 2011 in the United States alone) for use on livestock has increased to record numbers. Over 80 percent of all antibiotics produced worldwide go to food animals. Unfortunately most of these drugs were not sold to farmers to cure animals that had gotten sick. Rather most of these drugs were sold to make the animals grow faster and to suppress diseases from taking hold because of the alarmingly close animal quarters.

Farmers and ranchers discovered that small doses of antibiotics administered daily made most animals gain as much as 3 percent more weight than they otherwise would. More and more farmers and ranchers are using these drugs to promote artificial growth in their herds.

The problem is that we don't know enough about these drugs to know if they are safe. We do know that overuse of low-dose amounts of antibiotics in people, such as tetracycline, is leading to more and more drug-resistant strains of bacteria.

In addition to antibiotics, recombinant bovine growth hormone (rBGH or rBST) is injected into cows to make them produce more milk. This hormone causes health problems in cows. That increases the use of antibiotics on dairy farms even more. Studies show that rBGH poses a cancer-causing risk in humans. Yet, at the time this book went to print, the FDA does not require that products produced from cows that have been given rBST declare that on labels.

An Alkaline Diet

Over the past forty to fifty years, the science of nutrition has made great strides in understanding how the molecular makeup of foods affects our health. The only time we ever talked about alkaline and acid levels in the past was as it related to preserving a jar of homemade jam. Now we are hearing talk about the pH of our food and whether our bodies are acidic or alkaline.

Have you ever considered the pH of your food? It's actually quite important to think about pH levels in the foods that you eat. When your body's pH is out of balance, it becomes vulnerable to all sorts of ailments, including headaches, fatigue, inflammation, joint and muscle pain, skin problems, cancer, and a weakened immune system.

Let's take a step back. What is pH? The abbreviation pH is short for "potential of hydrogen." It's a measure of the acidity or alkalinity of our body's fluids and tissues. pH is measured on a scale from 0 to 14. The more acidic a solution is, the lower its pH. The more alkaline a solution is, the higher its pH. A pH of 7 is perfectly neutral. The healthiest pH for food is one that is slightly alkaline. Fruits and vegetables, especially those high in potassium, are more alkaline, and so they are natural neutralizers and lower your pH when you eat them. On the other hand, animal foods are more acidic, and when you eat them, they tend to raise your acidity levels. The good news is that eating a plant-based vegan diet will effortlessly increase the pH of your food, making it more alkaline, and therefore more healthful.

WHAT IS FOOD SCIENCE?

Food science is the application of basic sciences and engineering to study the physical, chemical, and biochemical nature of foods and the principles of food processing. It's amazing to realize that very few people know anything about food science, yet it is the very reason we have food on our grocery shelves.

Food science brings together multiple scientific disciplines. It incorporates concepts from fields such as microbiology, chemical engineering, packaging, preservation, and biochemistry.

It is because of the expansion of the study of food science, combined with the study of nutrition over the past forty to fifty years, that we now know much more about vitamins, minerals, and phytochemicals and how these micronutrients are used in our bodies.

Most people say that they don't like chemistry, don't understand it, and don't have anything to do with it. This is not true. Whether we know it or not, we live with and through chemistry every day. The human body is a living, breathing machine fueled by millions of chemical reactions every minute. Our health depends on whether those chemical reactions have what they need to create the products that make us healthy or make us sick.

After you eat, foods are broken down by your digestive system into single elements—such as oxygen, nitrogen, hydrogen, and carbon. Your body uses these elements for chemical reactions, such as giving you energy, growing your hair and nails, replacing old worn-out cells with new ones, and keeping your immune system strong and ready to attack germs, bacteria, and viruses that might invade your body.

The body is programed to keep us healthy. So when we make sure that we are fueling our bodies with food that works in concert with all of these chemical reactions, everything works right. We are specimens of health. On the other hand, when we eat foods that cause these reactions to use plan B and have to work much harder to rid our systems of too much sugar, fat, and toxins, the system eventually breaks down. We become sick.

The Truth behind Food Myths

With television, newspapers, magazines, and the Internet all shouting out different and conflicting information about health and nutrition, it's easy to get confused. Some myths have been perpetuated for so long that they're simply assumed to be true. Next, we discuss a few of the most common food myths out there and the truth behind them.

MYTH: EATING TOO MUCH SOY CAUSES BOYS TO GROW BOOBS

There is a lot of misinformation about soy out there. Will eating soy cause boys to grow breasts or reduce their testosterone levels? Can too much soy cause or cure cancer? Is genetically modified soy causing girls to start their menstrual cycles at younger ages? What are the benefits and dangers associated with soy protein?

According to the FDA, "25 grams of soy protein per day, as part of a diet low in saturated fat and cholesterol, may reduce the risk of heart disease." The good news is that organic soy products can add a heart-healthy dose of protein to one's diet. Study after study shows that eating a diet rich in foods that are low in saturated fats (such as soy) can help to reduce heart disease and lower blood cholesterol levels.

Soy, in particular, is especially well suited for this, because soy protein itself can directly lower LDL cholesterol levels by as much as 4 percent. Lunasin, which is a naturally occurring peptide in soy, disrupts the production of cholesterol in the liver and clears LDL cholesterol from the bloodstream.

Most soy foods also contain fiber. Plants are the only foods that contain fiber. Fiber has many very important roles, one of which is to stick to cholesterol, preventing it from being absorbed by the body.

Also, soy is a complete protein. That means it provides all eight of the essential amino acids needed for good health.

In addition, consuming one or two servings (up to 25 to 30 grams) of soy protein per day has been shown to promote bone strength. Protein helps with the production of collagen fibers that provide the framework for bones. A 2000 study conducted at Loma Linda University, a vegetarian promoting school in California, shows that in comparison with animal protein, soy protein decreases calcium excretion, a result of the lower sulfur amino acid content of soy protein. And, according to several large studies, adults over age eighty with low protein intake had much more rapid bone loss and a higher risk of fractures than those who ate plenty of soy.

While whole, organic, unprocessed soy foods can be very healthy for you, overly processed soy products—such as isolated proteins, oils, and flours—contain higher than normal levels of isoflavones in the form of phytoestrogens. These flours, powders, and oils are often used to make commercially prepared soy milk, veggie burgers, soy cheese, and many other overly processed imitation foods. In fact, it's pretty hard to find a processed food that doesn't contain some form of soy ingredient.

In moderation, these isoflavones can be beneficial, but in excess, these phytoestrogens can cause unintended side effects, such as mimicking human estrogen behaviors. This has actually been shown to be beneficial in reducing the symptoms of menopause in perimenopausal women, but it has also been shown to have negative effects in young girls and boys, possibly causing early menstruation in girls and mammary development in boys. However, these cases are rare and extreme, and they are caused by consuming very large amounts of highly processed non-organic soy products, including soy protein isolates.

These overly processed soy foods also contain high levels of phytic acid, or phytates, which block the absorption of essential minerals such as calcium, magnesium, iron, and especially zinc in the intestinal tract. Overly processed soy foods also contain trypsin inhibitors and hemagglutinin that can stunt human growth.

As you can see, there are many benefits to consuming a diet containing soy protein. Just remember to buy and consume whole foods and foods that are minimally processed. When consuming soy products, stick with soy nuts, edamame, fermented tofu products, and soy milks that do not contain sugars and oils.

In addition to eating a diet with soy protein, adding a variety of vegetables, fruits, grains, and legumes will ensure you get the necessary nutrients from your heart-healthy, meat-free diet. Replacing foods heavy in cholesterol and saturated fats with whole unprocessed soy foods such as edamame and fermented soy products such as tempeh and miso, can lead to better overall health.

MYTH: MILK, IT DOES A BODY GOOD

Really? That's not what studies show.

Did you know that humans are the only species on the planet that drink milk from another mammal for sustenance? Who perpetuates the myth that milk makes strong bones? Big Dairy, that's who. And why are millions of people feeding their precious babies what just might be the worst possible food on the planet?

Back in the 1950s, the government decided that milk was the "perfect food." Since then, the lobbyists behind the dairy industry have worked day and night, spending millions of dollars to convince us that milk is good for us.

The truth is, cow's milk *is* the perfect food—for baby cows! Just as a human mother's milk is the perfect food for human babies, mother's milk from all mammals is designed for two main purposes: to nourish the offspring and to promote bonding between mother and child.

Mother's milk provides high levels of nutrition to a newborn: carbohydrates, proteins, fats, and yes, calcium. All mammalian species produce milk, but the composition of milk for each species varies widely. Other kinds of milk are very different from human breast milk. When we compare the digestive system of a cow with the digestive system of a human, they're opposite. Cows have four stomachs and 4 feet (1.21 m) of intestine. On the other hand, humans have one stomach and 27 feet (8.23 m) of intestine. The type of food we eat and the way we digest are dramatically different.

Whole cow's milk contains too little iron, retinol, vitamin E, vitamin C, vitamin D, unsaturated fats, and essential fatty acids for human babies. In addition, it takes a lot of naturally occurring growth hormones in the cow's milk to turn that 25-pound (11.34 kg) calf into a huge 600-pound (272 kg) cow. Those hormones were never intended to go into a human child. Whole cow's milk also contains too much protein, sodium, potassium, phosphorus, and chloride, which may put a strain on an infant's immature kidneys. In addition, the proteins, fats, and calcium in whole cow's milk are more difficult for an infant to digest and absorb than the ones in breast milk. Some infants are allergic to one or more of the components of cow's milk, and most often, the cow's milk proteins. That should come as no surprise, because it was never designed for human babies. Human milk is for human babies, and cow's milk is for cow babies.

The problem of drinking cow's milk doesn't go away as a baby grows. The sugar in milk is called lactose. Infants' intestinal villi produce lactase, which is an enzyme secreted specifically to break down lactose. As the baby grows, the production of lactase decreases, and the baby begins to naturally deny the breast in favor of solid foods. Once the production of lactase declines, milk drinking should also cease.

However, the dairy industry has done such a good job of promoting its product that we've forced our bodies to drink milk and digest it throughout childhood and into adulthood. For many people, this causes great discomfort, otherwise known as lactose intolerance. The real truth is that we are all lactose intolerant, but force-feeding our bodies dairy has created an artificial tolerance to the stuff.

We mentioned that the other reason babies drink milk is to promote the bonding between mother and child. The bonding between mother and child during nursing happens due to the protein casein. Casein, like other opiates such as morphine and heroin, creates a euphoric effect that is highly addictive. The baby literally becomes addicted to mother's milk. This addiction promotes bonding, and it also ensures the nourishment of the baby.

As the baby grows and thrives, he needs to wean from the breast, both emotionally and physically, the same way a drug-addicted person must wean from the drug.

Big Dairy is literally a drug dealer, pushing milk on babies, children, and adults, lying to us, telling us that their product is "good" for us. For many years now, doctors have known that dairy causes inflammation in human bodies. Often when a person goes to the doctor with the first signs of arthritis, the doctor recommends that the patient stop consuming dairy products because the consumption of dairy creates inflammation. According to the Physician's Committee for Responsible Medicine, the types of proteins in dairy foods can cause irritation in the tissue around joints, leading to increased arthritic pain. Unfortunately, many Western doctors are not often given much training in the study of nutrition, sometimes as little as a four-hour lecture in their entire course of study.

In addition, the protein in dairy milk, casein, which makes up 80 to 87 percent of cow's milk, has been found in numerous research papers, to promote many types of cancers.

Also, as we mentioned earlier, animal proteins—such as those found in dairy, meat, chicken, and eggs—are high in a certain type of acid. When consumed, particularly in large amounts as in the Sickness and Disease-promoting diet the acid causes a condition in the human body called "metabolic acidosis." Research over the past few years has shown that cancers grow and thrive in acidic conditions.

This high level of acid also accounts for the fact that countries with the highest intake of dairy products also have the highest rates of osteoporosis leading to bone fractures. "What," you say, "we thought that milk was good for bones." Well, the human body is designed to be alkaline. So when the body becomes acidic, this wonderful healing machine goes to work to correct the problem. The body uses minerals to neutralize the acid and return your body to alkaline. Let's take a wild guess at which minerals it uses. You guessed it, calcium and phosphorous! And where does the body get that calcium and phosphorous? Yes, the bones! So instead of milk making your bones strong, it actually leaches calcium from your bones and weakens them. So you make the call: Does this sound like milk "does our bodies good"?

MYTH: ATHLETES NEED MEAT FOR PEAK PERFORMANCE

Try to tell that to mixed martial arts fighter Jake Shields, bodybuilder Jim Morris, or power-lifter Bill McCarthy. You also might want to mention it to four-time Chicago Golden Glove title holder Amanda Reister, NASCAR driver Leilani Munter, soccer Olympian Kara Lang, extreme distance runner Vidal Ixel, mixed martial artist Mac Danzig, or figure skater Meagan Duhamel.

Super strong, super elite, and super vegan, these athletes prove that meat isn't needed for optimum athletic performance. Furthermore, athletes who eat a plant-based diet claim they have faster recovery times and more energy, and they say that they eat a wider variety of foods than they did prior to going vegan.

MYTH: THE INCREDIBLE EDIBLE EGG

Eggs have gotten both a bad rap and a good rap, nutritionally, in recent history. Here's the truth: Eggs are not meant for human consumption. That is why they are responsible for the second most common food allergy, second only to cow's milk. Sure, eggs contain a lot of nutrition. Eggs contain all of the nutrition necessary to take an embryo to a fully autonomous fluffy, feathery, little baby chicken, ready to leave the nest in only a few days.

It takes a hen about 25 hours to produce a single egg. During this time, the mother hen uses up many of her resources, especially calcium from her bones to make that shell, to make sure that egg has all of the protein, vitamins, minerals, and fat needed for her chick to properly develop. If left to her own devices, that mother would then eat that egg to regain those resources once she realizes the egg is not fertilized.

In addition to the nutrition in an egg, it also contains 182 milligrams of cholesterol and 5 grams of fat in only 72 calories. In fact, eggs are mostly fat and protein, and you can get all the fat and protein you need from vegan sources that are healthier.

To make matters worse, the proteins in fatty egg yolks can overstimulate your immune system, causing your body to produce excess mucus, fever, fatigue, and pain. Eggs can also slow down your digestion and elimination, leading to that feeling of being "clogged up."

MYTH: HUMANS ARE BORN TO EAT MEAT

We hear this one all the time. The truth is: The human body thrives on a diet of plant foods. We are natural herbivores.

Our bodies are not at all well adapted to eating animals. Humans have hands that are useful for gathering vegetables and fruits, but aren't that good for killing and ripping skin and flesh. And, unlike natural carnivores and omnivores, we do not feel the natural instinct to catch other living animals for food. Natural carnivores (cats, for example) will see a mouse or bird and immediately begin to hunt it. And if they catch it, they will dismember it and eat it raw.

Human canine teeth are small and blunt, and we have flat molars for grinding up plant fibers. Look at the teeth of natural carnivores and omnivores such as dogs or cats, and you'll see long, pointed canine teeth for catching prey and tearing the hide, and sharp-edged teeth in the back for shearing off chunks of flesh.

Furthermore, our digestive systems are much better designed to digest plant foods. The carbohydrate-digesting enzymes produced in our mouths and our long intestinal tracts are that of natural herbivores.

MYTH: VEGANS CAN'T EAT ENOUGH PROTEIN

Protein is one of the macronutrients (carbohydrates and fats being the other two) that are essential for our bodies to take in on a daily basis to function properly. But how much protein do we really need, and which are the best sources?

The macronutrient protein was discovered in 1839 by a Dutch chemist named Gerhard Mulder. He named it proteios, which is a Greek word meaning "of prime importance." You will see why in a moment.

Proteins are composed of long chains of hundreds or even thousands of amino acids linked together. These amino acids are made up of carbon, hydrogen, oxygen, and nitrogen. The nitrogen is what makes the protein structure different from carbohydrates and fats, which are made from carbon, hydrogen, and oxygen. Fats and carbohydrates can be stored in the body, but amino acids cannot because there are no specialized cells in the body that can act as reservoirs.

Scientists have identified more than 500 amino acids. Of these, only twenty-two are proteinogenic (protein building). Twenty of these are genetically encoded in the body, while the other two are synthetically produced. So when you hear people talk about amino acids, they're usually referring to the twenty standard amino acids. Of these twenty, eleven are made by the body, so we don't have to worry about getting them from our food. Because our bodies do not make the remaining nine, they are referred to as "essential" amino acids. We need to make sure we eat foods that contain these nine.

How these twenty-two amino acids are linked together determines the type of protein and what it does in the body. There are hundreds of thousands of different proteins to accommodate all of the needed proteins in the body. Proteins are required for the structure, function, and regulation of the body's cells, tissues, and organs, and each protein has unique functions. Examples of proteins are hormones, enzymes, and antibodies.

All foods contain some protein, some carbohydrate, and some fat. Yes, even 15 percent of the calories from broccoli comes from fat. But don't use that as an excuse to avoid eating broccoli! Fifty-seven percent of the calories from spinach are from protein; however, it is not protein that contains all nine of the essential amino acids, or what is commonly called a "complete" protein. This is where the argument starts, with people thinking that it is vital that we eat animal proteins because they contain all of the essential amino acids, making meat a "complete protein."

But here is the hole in that theory: At one time it was thought that you needed to eat a food that had all the essential amino acids in it for your body to get a "complete" protein. However, research now shows us that as long as you consume all the essential amino acids *throughout the day,* you're covered for your required protein needs. So consuming a variety of whole (not processed) plant foods will provide enough of all of the essential amino acids needed for human health.

In addition, when consuming plants for protein, you'll also get fiber, vitamins, minerals, and phytochemicals along with the protein. When consuming animal proteins, a person does get a complete protein, but very little to no vitamins and minerals, absolutely no fiber, and no phytochemicals. (We'll discuss what these are and how much we need later.) When animal proteins are eaten in large amounts in the Sickness and Disease-promoting diet a person gets a very high percentage of saturated fat and cholesterol and high amounts of acid. This elevated blood acid rate has been shown in numerous studies to create the perfect environment for different types of cancers to grow and thrive.

The *American Journal of Clinical Nutrition* says 2.5 percent of our daily calories should come from protein. According to the World Health Organization, it's about 5 percent. After forty years of research, Dr. Colin Campbell, author of the *The China Study,* agrees that only 5 percent—and no more than 10 percent—of calories should come from animal proteins. It's interesting to note that 6 percent of the calories in human mother's milk is composed of protein. So if nature tells us that we only need 6 percent of our calories from protein during the time of our life when we are growing and developing the fastest, why in the world would we think we need 30 percent or more of our calories coming from protein when we're older? What people get when they eat animal proteins is a very high percentage of saturated fat and cholesterol and acidic blood levels, particularly when animal proteins are eaten as the largest component of every meal.

So what does 5 percent to 10 percent of our daily calories look like? Proteins have 4 calories per gram. For an example, let's calculate 5 percent protein for a male consuming 3,000 calories/day:

Step One: 5 percent of 3,000 = 150 calories

Step Two: 150 calories × (1 gram divided by 4 calories) = 37.5 g (about 38 grams)

Now let's calculate 5 percent protein for a woman consuming 2,000 calories per day:

Step One: 5 percent of 2,000 = 100 calories

Step Two: 100 calories × (1 gram divided by 4 calories) = 25 g

That's a lot lower than the Western average of 100 grams a day, that's for sure.

"To consume a diet that contains enough, but not too much, protein, simply replace animal products with grains, vegetables, legumes (peas, beans, and lentils), and fruits," clarifies the Physician's Committee for Responsible Medicine. "As long as one is eating a variety of plant foods in sufficient quantity to maintain one's weight, the body gets plenty of protein."

SAMPLE PARTIAL DAILY PROTEIN INTAKE

Food	Protein (g)
Oatmeal (1 cup, or 80 g)	6
Banana, apple, strawberries (1 cup, or 150 g each)	3
Salad: 1 cup (67 g) kale, 1 cup (30 g) spinach, ½ cup (25 g) sun-dried tomatoes, and ½ (70 g) cup cucumbers	12
Beans, adzuki (1 cup, or 256 g)	17
Steamed broccoli, green and yellow squash (½ cup, or 35 g, each)	7
Total	45

As you can see by the table above, it is almost impossible to develop a protein deficiency unless a person is consuming a calorie-deficient diet. Excess protein consumption is stressful to the body because protein is not readily usable for fuel and must be excreted. The nitrogen that accompanies protein is released into the body and causes byproducts such as urea and ammonia that must be detoxified by the liver and kidneys.

Nitrogen must be released from the amino acid chains to convert protein to carbohydrate or fat that can be used for energy. The body is meant to get its fuel from *carbohydrates*, not protein. Therefore, on a high-protein diet, the body cannot efficiently or effectively convert the protein into energy.

We mentioned how a diet high in animal protein raises the acid level of our bodies. When we consume more than 10 percent of our daily calories from animal proteins, this acid level sets up the perfect environment for cancers to grow. We also mentioned that our bodies like to be alkaline, and we think everyone is aware of the many types of new drinking waters that boast higher pH levels. Later we'll take a look at what all this information about acid, alkaline, and pH in water means.

What Foods Are Good for Me?

Today, people have so many questions about food and nutrition. Should I take a multivitamin? What is an omega-3 and where do I get it? How much protein do I need and what are the best sources? Yet, fifty years ago, no one was asking any of these questions. How did we go from families that chose their foods from simple basic food groups in the 1950s (see chart below) to trying to understand the massive amount of dietary information we now receive on a daily basis?

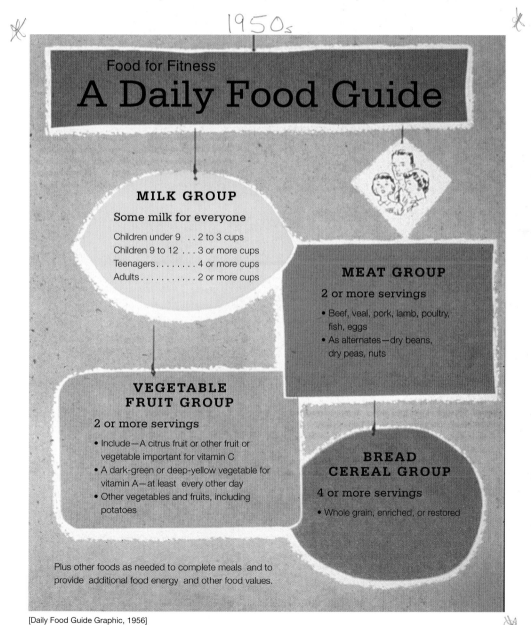

Food for Fitness
A Daily Food Guide

MILK GROUP

Some milk for everyone

Children under 9 . . 2 to 3 cups
Children 9 to 12 . . . 3 or more cups
Teenagers . . . . 4 or more cups
Adults . . . . 2 or more cups

MEAT GROUP

2 or more servings

- Beef, veal, pork, lamb, poultry, fish, eggs
- As alternates—dry beans, dry peas, nuts

VEGETABLE FRUIT GROUP

2 or more servings

- Include—A citrus fruit or other fruit or vegetable important for vitamin C
- A dark-green or deep-yellow vegetable for vitamin A—at least every other day
- Other vegetables and fruits, including potatoes

BREAD CEREAL GROUP

4 or more servings

- Whole grain, enriched, or restored

Plus other foods as needed to complete meals and to provide additional food energy and other food values.

[Daily Food Guide Graphic, 1956]

As the knowledge of nutrition and the important role that food plays in our health has increased over the past sixty years, the social, economic, and health conditions in our world have also changed. The typical family in the 1950s included two parents, and the majority, if not all, of the meals were prepared and eaten at home with the entire family present. Today, the typical family is more likely to consist of either a two-parent household where both parents work full-time or a household with a single parent working two or more jobs to keep food on the table. Add to this the busy school and extracurricular activities of children and caretaking of aging parents, you have family situations that leave little to no time for meal preparation, and very rarely does the whole family dine together. This time-challenged family dynamic has turned the small mom-and-pop-owned corner stores and restaurants of sixty years ago into large worldwide conglomerates that offer quick, easy, inexpensive meal options to help these overburdened families.

One example of the food industry's first offerings to busy, overburdened families was the American TV dinner offered in the 1950s. Since then, the food industry has grown tremendously, offering thousands of processed and ready-to-eat meals in grocery stores, as well as expanding into the overabundance of international fast food chains. Worldwide food sales have skyrocketed. And even though we are experiencing a worldwide economic depression food industry sales are at an all-time high. When looking at the money that is at stake here, it is easy to see how the food industry has turned into big business competing for our hard-earned money capitalizing on our daily need to eat.

Unfortunately, over the past 50 years, we've trusted that the food industry was developing new and convenient foods with our best interest and health in mind, but nothing could be further from the truth. Instead, we gave control of the food we eat to a monetarily driven industry by assuming that these companies would never sell us anything that would be detrimental to our health. If someone came up to you and said, "Here try this," what is the first thing you would say? Most people would ask, "What is it?" Yet each and every day, most people walk into grocery stores and purchase products without looking at the ingredients or asking, "What is in this?" We assume that because it is packaged and on the shelf that it is safe and good for us. As we can see from the current state of the world's health, this attitude has not served us well. In fact, it has caused us to become a very sick world.

The food industry cannot be the only ones to blame for the over-processed and-disease-promoting foods we are now eating. The food industry in each country is monitored, following guidelines and labeling regulations set forth by their particular governing agencies. For example, in the United States the Food and Drug Administration establishes and enforces all rules, regulations, and requirements for food ingredients and packaging for packaged foods. In Canada, there are two federal departments, Health Canada and the Canadian Food Inspection Agency (CFIA), in Europe it is the European Commission (EC), in Japan it is the Ministry of Health, Labour and Welfare (MHLW), etc. While the initial reasons for government agencies becoming involved in the monitoring of our food were and are well intentioned and for the "good of the people," that has definitely changed over the years.

Today, the influence of big business has caused our government and the laws they enact to become nutritionally misguided. Numerous government agencies around the world have come under scrutiny for placing people in these agencies that have ties to the food industry, resulting in very large conflicts of interest. For example, recommendations for which foods Americans should eat comes from the National Academy of Sciences (NAS). Today, although the NAS still accepts public donations, it is funded by food companies. The NAS invites food industry experts to sit on its board, help review the latest findings in nutrition, and then make recommendations for Americans' dietary consumption. While it seems like industry experts would be the ideal people to review research and make recommendation for food consumption, there is a problem. The food industry representatives who are asked to participate on panels are from the very companies that would stand to profit from the recommendations that will be made to the public.

In Europe, the EFSA is responsible for scientific advice on the safety of pesticides, genetically modified organisms (GMOs), and food additives. These recommendations are designed to protect the safety of the public's health. However, an article published in June 2011 by the Corporate European Observatory (CEO), revealed that the EFSA and the other EU agencies were being investigated by the European Court of Auditors over alleged conflicts of interest. CEO also identified conflicts of interest among the members of the EFSA panel on food additives and nutrient sources in food (ANS panel) by uncovering evidence of incomplete declarations of outside interests, which suggested further possible conflicts of interest. CEO stated that if the new rules established by the European Medicines Agency (EMA) in 2011 were applied at EFSA, four of the experts on the ANS panel would be disqualified from sitting on the panel. The CEO also stated that the ANS panel had also been criticized for publishing controversial "scientific opinions" on certain food additives, including aspartame and artificial colorants when several of these substances have been found to provoke allergies or are suspected to be carcinogenic.

In addition to recommendations on what we should eat, our government agencies also write and enforce the laws applying to the information printed on our food packages, nutritional labels, and determine what types of health claims can be made about the food we purchase. While our governments definitely play a vital role in keeping some potentially dangerous products off the market, there is still plenty of opportunity for food manufacturers to use these rules to deceive and mislead customers about products. For example, we have all seen packages proclaiming that a product is "low fat" or "low sodium." But what exactly does that mean? The food manufacturer counts on you thinking that it means their product is low in fat and sodium, but that isn't always true. The fat and sodium levels may be lower than in another product, but still way too high.

Also, did you know that some governments allow companies to round the amounts on nutritional labels? For example, a product may have 0.45 grams per serving of trans fat in the product. Hopefully we all know by now that trans fats (products made with hydrogenated oils) are bad, and we shouldn't ever eat foods with trans fats in them. However, because a government allows the manufacturer to round number on the nutritional label, the 0.45 grams per serving can be rounded down to zero. Therefore the customer thinks the product they are buying had no trans fats when, in fact, it contains trans fats. You would argue that 0.45 grams may not be a lot, but remember that number is per the serving size. If you eat more than one serving (and most of us do), you will have exceeded the amount of trans fats that is safe to have in your diet, which again is zero.

The food on supermarket shelves, nutritional information on packages, and big business-influenced government dietary recommendations are not the only ways in which the food we eat is being manipulated and misrepresented to consumers. The way our food is grown and developed is also being affected and changed without the consumer's knowledge or consent, which we will cover later in this book.

Now that you have a basic understanding and awareness of what has happened to our food supply over the past fifty years, and how it has impacted the current state of our health, we can show how all the pieces come together to give you a new appreciation for how our bodies function, what type of food is necessary to nourish our bodies, and how a vegan or plant-based diet fits right into that equation. And in the chapters to come, we will explore how our food choices affect our health—and the very world we live in.

Getting Started

We hope that after reading the previous pages, you have a lot of good reasons and the motivation to make some choices in your life that will help you achieve a healthier you and a healthier planet. Gerrie can't remember where she heard or saw this quote, but it is another reason for us to care about what we eat: "Anything that has the power to make you sick also has the power to make you well."

We don't recommend that you try to totally change your current way of eating and living all at once. Going "cold turkey" (no pun intended) and becoming a WellBeing (WeBe) all at once is just too big a step. The convenience-oriented, fast-food society we live in will provide little to no support for your new habits, and you will become frustrated, give up, and never achieve your health goals. So we have put together some steps that may help you get to your goal in an achievable way. These are only meant to be suggestions to help you on this journey. If you find other ways of achieving the goals of eating a plant-based diet; cutting out refined, processed, and extracted foods; and living in a way that improves the well-being of our planet and our lives, then by all means do whatever works for you.

Next, we offer a simple philosophy for going vegan and our easy ten-step process.

OUR PHILOSOPHY: REPLACE, DON'T DENY

Today's world is full of don'ts, such as don't eat trans fats, don't drink soda, don't eat fried foods, and don't eat fast food. Making major changes in your lifestyle, as in changing the way you eat, is very rarely done successfully by approaching it in an exclusionary way. When we try to change our eating patterns by telling ourselves what we *can't* eat, we automatically feel deprived, rebellious, and unhappy. So here's our simple philosophy: It is more successful to start out by asking, "What can I eat?" and approach this journey from a place of choosing what you *can* eat. Think of this as a "replacement" way of eating, not a "denial" way of eating.

So what do we need to eat? The more we study nutrition and its relationship to our health, the more we are convinced that it is more common sense than science. Wouldn't it make sense that if we eat the foods that supply us with what our bodies need to function properly, our bodies will work better?

Take our cars, for example. If we put the right type of octane fuel, oil, and other fluids in our cars, then they run right. If we swap out the fuel for another type of fuel, or if we don't replenish the fluids or keep the levels at the proper amounts, then our cars break down.

This is true for all living beings—plants and animals. We've seen it with factory farmed cows. Now that they are being fed corn and other non-vegetation ingredients, such as ground-up meats that were not fit for human consumption, the cows have developed mad cow disease and very high levels of *E. coli* bacteria. Cows are meant to eat grass! When they eat the way nature intended, their bodies work properly and there is very little *E. coli* found in the meat.

The human body is no different. Research has shown that our genes affect only 2 to 3 percent of our health. The remaining 97 to 98 percent of the illnesses and infirmities we experience come from our environment and the choices we make. It is true that our genes may give us a predisposition to different types of health conditions, but the choices we make determine whether we prevent those conditions from happening, or encourage them.

The human body is an amazing healing machine. It's hardwired to heal itself. But even the human body has its limits. If we work in concert with the way our bodies are designed to eat, and not against it, our bodies can keep us healed and whole.

OUR TEN STEPS TO A HEALTHIER YOU

What steps can you take to experience a healthy coexistence with your body? We have broken it down into ten simple steps that you can do one at a time, or as many as you can successfully handle at once, and be successful. Once you have mastered one, then move on to the next.

1. Add more greens into your diet. Some of the heartier leafy greens or as some have called them, "angry" lettuces—such as kale, collard, turnip, chard, and mustard greens—are very important for us to eat every day. For every one calorie you ingest of these greens, you get a dose of all the daily essential vitamins, minerals, and phytochemicals your body needs. The only reason we can't live only on greens is because they are so low in calories, you can't eat enough to sustain yourself. Other leafy greens that are also little powerhouses of vitamins, minerals, and phytochemicals are spinach and bok choy.

So how do you add these wonderful superfoods into your diet? You don't need to just eat salads to get your greens. Simply add greens to everything. For example, put greens in your morning smoothie, have spinach enchiladas with red sauce (and no cheese), or add greens to your soups, stews, burritos, tacos, sandwiches, or pita pockets. Leafy greens sure pack a powerful nutrient punch. Just by adding more greens into your diet, we guarantee that you will feel a difference within a week!

2. Replace animal proteins with plant proteins. We love plant proteins such as legumes, beans, lentils, and peas. Depending on how much animal protein you now eat, start by cutting back on the number of times you eat it a day or a week. For example, if you eat animal protein at every meal (and the majority of us do because it is the center of our plates), cut back to once a day. If you eat animal proteins once a day, cut back to only two or three times a week.

At your meatless meals, simply add 1 cup (about 240 g) of beans, lentils, or peas to your dish. Just like adding greens, adding beans will not really change the overall flavor of your dish, but it will definitely give you the protein you need along with fiber, and without all of the fat, calories, and cholesterol that's in animal protein. As long as you prepare the beans in the manner we suggest and use them in the proper amount, you will not suffer from the dreaded "intestinal discomfort" (flatulence) that so many people dislike.

3. Replace dairy with plant milks and cheese substitutes. Some of our favorite plant milks are almond, oat, soy, cashew, coconut, rice, and hemp. For cheese substitutes, we suggest soy or nut based "cheese" and we love the soy-and-gluten-free tapioca-based products. There are so many plant milk options that we're sure you will find one that you like. Just make sure that the plant milk you choose is unsweetened to avoid processed sugars. Plus, that way it works well in both sweet and savory applications.

Using plant milk is simple; just use it as you would cow's milk. Pour a plant milk over your cereal, in your glass, or in your recipe instead of cow's, goat's, or sheep's milk. In most uses, you won't even notice a difference. The same goes for nondairy cheeses. Add a slice to your sandwich, melt it over nachos, sprinkle it on salads, and top your pizza with it, just as you would an animal-based cheese.

4. Replace overly processed foods with minimally cooked whole plant foods. This step is a little harder for people to adopt than the others because it takes a little bit of planning, which is something most of us don't take the time to do. This new way of eating is not hard. It's just different. With a little effort and planning, you will find it easy, cheaper, and more delicious.

This step is all about eating foods that are as close to their natural state as possible. For example, incorporate apples into your diet instead of applesauce or apple juice. This will provide you with more nutrients, more fiber, and less sugar. Instead of purchasing pre-made soups in cans, break out the slow cooker and make your own soups and stews from scratch. Store and restaurant soups and stews are usually loaded with sodium, oils, and other unwanted ingredients, such as preservatives and sugars. Avoid buying foods that come in boxes, bags, or cans unless they have five or fewer ingredients and do not contain unwanted ingredients. For example, Gerrie's favorite tomato product is aseptically packaged, and the ingredients label reads: tomatoes. (See chapter 5 for more information on reading and deciphering labels.)

We know that in the busy world we live in, it is almost impossible to avoid boxes, bags, and cans entirely, and we certainly don't. We recommend that instead of heating up pre-made frozen meals, you do a little planning and do batch cooking on the weekends or when you have time. Make enough when you cook to have leftovers for another meal or freeze some. We believe in cooking once and eating two or three times. Swap out products such as protein bars for some homemade yummy oat bars or homemade granolas that are much healthier and do not contain fractionated soy and other overprocessed ingredients.

5. Replace processed sugars with fruits and fruit juices in recipes. Refined sugars have absolutely no nutritional value at all—no vitamins, minerals, phytochemicals, or fiber. They are simply junk food, and they have no place in our diets. By replacing sugars with fruits and fruit juices—such as dates and prunes—you'll add vitamins and minerals, and, in the case of whole fruits, you'll get fiber as well.

This is actually one of the easier steps. Simply use blended dates (date paste; see the recipe on page 145), applesauce, prunes, or apples in place of sugars in recipes. (See chapter 5 for more information on substituting sugars with fruits and fruit juices in recipes.)

6. Replace extracted oils with foods that have oils in them. Extracted oils are nothing more than fat that has been extracted from a plant. Did you know that it takes approximately forty-four olives to make 1 tablespoon (15 ml) of olive oil? Would you ever sit down and eat forty-four olives all at once? Plus when you eat an olive, you're getting fiber, vitamins, and minerals along with the fat in the correct concentration. One tablespoon of oil contains 120 calories, and all 120 calories are from fat!

In addition to the concentrated intake of fat, oils are a highly concentrated and often hidden source of calories. If you consumed only 3 tablespoons (45 ml) of oil a day (the Sickness and Disease-promoting diet contains a lot more than 3 tablespoons (45 ml) because oils are in almost everything), you would be consuming 360 calories a day that are nothing but fat. If you multiply that by seven days in a week, you would be taking in 2,520 calories in one week that come from just fat in your food. For a woman, that is more than one day's worth of calories.

Oils are also high in omega-6 fatty acids. Omega-6s are essential in our diets, but they are plentiful in a plant-based diet, and when converted in the body, they create inflammation. Our bodies produce a limited amount of the enzyme that converts omega-3s and -6s, so when we eat too many omega-6s, they use up the conversion enzyme, and then little to no omega-3s are converted. We then end up with inflammation in the body. So instead of eating oil, we recommend eating the food that the oil comes from instead, such as avocados, olives, nuts, and seeds. This way, you get the right amount of oil, along with fiber, vitamins, minerals, and phytochemicals.

Don't worry about how you will cook without oil. Sautéing is easily accomplished using water, vegetable broth, and even wine! After all, the purpose of the oil is to keep things from sticking to the bottom of the pot, and we have discovered that any other liquid serves the same purpose.

7. Replace sodium with citrus juices, sodium-free dried vegetables, and other seasonings. The taste buds measuring sour and salty are right next to each other on the tongue. If you add citrus such as lemon juice or lime juice, your taste buds are tricked into thinking that sodium has been added to the food. This will add flavor and satisfy your "taste" for salt without the negative effects.

8. Eat only 100 percent *whole* grains. Over the past twenty years, we have been consuming more and more cereals, breads, and overly processed products that use cheaper enriched, processed, and refined grains that have higher gluten levels than whole grains. High gluten ingredients are used in more than just baked goods, too. Many prepackaged seasonings, broths, dressings, sauces, and other processed foods listing "natural flavors" contained refined gluten. People are unknowingly eating far more gluten than our predecessors. Gerrie believes that the combination of eating overly processed, nutrient-less and fiber-less grains, and not eating fresh fruits and vegetables is one reason so many people are becoming intolerant to wheat and other grains.

Our bodies are meant to eat whole grains that contain fiber and nutrients. So make sure that any grain product you consume is made from 100 percent *whole*, organic, and/or sprouted grains.

Beware of products boasting "made with whole grains." That just means that some of the grains in the product are whole, but not all of them. Be a label reader.

9. Eat three to five servings of fruit a day. This step requires the least preparation, and it's the most convenient. But surprisingly very few people actually do it each day. Eat a piece of fruit as a snack, put fresh berries on your cereal in the morning, or cut up some mangoes, watermelon, or pineapple for dessert.

10. Eat 1 ounce (28 g) of raw nuts and seeds each day. Nuts and seeds are very nutritious. They should be in your diet every day to help boost your immune system.

Make sure they are raw and not oiled and salted. When nuts and seeds are oiled, salted, roasted, and toasted, the grams of fat and milligrams of sodium are drastically increased, and the nutrients are decreased. For example, 1 ounce (28 g) of raw cashews has 12 grams of fat and 3 milligrams of sodium, but 1 ounce (28 g) of roasted cashews with oil has 62 grams of fat and 86 milligrams of sodium. Also in this small portion, the amount of iron drops 1 percent of the daily recommended requirements. Dry-roasted is acceptable from time to time.

While nuts and seeds are very nutritious and good for you, they also contain a lot of calories, and many nuts have a very high ratio of omega-6 fatty acids to omega-3s. So enjoy raw nuts, but make sure to limit them to 1 ounce (28 g)—or maybe 2 ounces (56 g)—a day.

That is so much information! We have packed the rest of this book with even more information, tips, tricks, resources, recipes, meal plans, and more to make your switch to vegan as easy as possible.

We are here to help guide you through your adventure, and hundreds of thousands of people are also on this path. You can meet them at community potlucks, get-togethers, online chat rooms, veg festivals, and other events. There are so many ways to connect with other like-minded WeBes, so let's get started!

Chapter 2

Do It for the Environment!

A good question to ask any self-proclaimed environmentalist is, "Do you eat meat?" If the answer is yes, be ready to have a nice long discussion with that well-meaning individual about how veganism is environmentalism.

Eating a vegan diet is truly the easiest way to work toward a greener future. Because the amount of energy and land used for the factory farming of animals for food is an unsustainable way to feed the planet, eating a diet full of nutritious plant foods will reduce your carbon footprint, and it will also help to create a greener future for generations to come.

The Impact of Factory Farming on the Environment

Animal agriculture—the raising of animals such as cows, chickens, pigs, and even fish—has a tremendous impact on our environment. Let's talk about each type in turn.

BEEF, POULTRY, AND PORK FARMING

Did you know it takes the equivalent of 55 calories of energy to raise just 1 calorie of energy from beef? Livestock farming has a devastating effect on the environment. Here's why.

Destroying the rainforest: Worldwide, factory farming is taking a toll on the environment. Each year Central America imports more than 200 million pounds (90 million kg) of beef to the United States. In 2013, Japan imports of US beef increased by 52 percent. England imports much of its beef from Argentina, Brazil, and Uruguay. Worldwide meat production has tripled over the last four decades and increased 20 percent in just the past 10 years. Approximately 56 billion land animals are reared and slaughtered for human consumption annually, and livestock inventories are expected to double by 2050, with most increases occurring in the developing world, according to the Food and Agricultural Organization (FAO) of the United Nations.

Let's put fuel costs and pollution aside. Where does all of this beef come from? The grazing land needed to raise these cattle is often found by clear-cutting dense rainforest land. Studies estimate that the necessity for more grazing land means that for every minute of every day, a land area equivalent to seven football fields is destroyed in the Amazon basin. For each hamburger that originates from animals raised on rainforest land, approximately 55 square feet (16.76 sq m) of rainforest had to be destroyed. According to a 1997 study, farm animals and animal production facilities cover one-third of the planet's land surface, using more than two-thirds of all available agricultural land *including* the land needed to grow crops for animal feed. It's not just the rainforest. More than 260 million acres of national forests have already been clear-cut for animal agriculture. With increased per capita meat consumption, and an ever-growing population, we can only expect to see more deforestation in the future.

Harming native wildlife: Clear-cutting of forests is only one aspect of the devastating ecological effects livestock grazing has to the native wilderness. For example, in the United States, it is still legal within the national park system. It is actually subsidized by taxpayer dollars, at an alarming rate of more than $100 million per year, to have privately owned cattle graze on publicly owned lands. Native species, such as the desert tortoise, the pronghorn antelope, and many species of birds suffer. Livestock grazing currently has a negative effect on 22 percent of the species on the threatened and endangered species list.

Wasting water: In addition to needing land for raising meat, animal agriculture also requires water. The amount of water needed for animal consumption is almost equivalent to all other uses of water, *combined*. To grow 1 pound (455 g) of beef requires about 2,500 gallons (9.5 kl) of water. Compare that to 1 pound (455 g) of soy, which only requires 250 gallons (946 L), or 1 pound of wheat, only 25 gallons (95 L). It is inefficient use of resources, because it takes years to grow that single pound of beef. The amount of water needed to produce just one hamburger is enough to take a nice long, hot shower every day for 2½ weeks. With numbers like these, eating vegan is surely the green way to go.

Manure pollution: Beyond the waste, there is water pollution. Agricultural pesticides and manure seep into the groundwater, eventually finding their way to the rivers and oceans. Specifically on farms, the manure contains high levels of oxygen-demanding substances. According to the Environmental Protection Agency (EPA), "When discharged to surface water, the biodegradable material (manure) is decomposed by aquatic bacteria and other microorganisms. During this process, dissolved oxygen is consumed, reducing the amount available for aquatic animals. Severe depressions in dissolved oxygen levels can result in fish kills." There are numerous examples of fish kills resulting from manure discharges and runoff from various types of Concentrated Animal Feeding Operations (CAFOs).

Fecal waste may be deposited directly into surface waters by grazing animals. Manually collected manure may also be introduced into surface waters. This is typically via storage structure failure, overflow, or operator error.

Manure can also enter surface waters via runoff if it is over applied or misapplied to land. For example, manure application to saturated or frozen soils may result in a discharge to surface waters. Factors that promote runoff to surface waters are steep land slope, high rainfall, low soil porosity, and proximity to surface water.

Air polluting: Air pollution is another negative environmental impact. On hot, humid days, the odor of waste lagoons is detectable up to ½ mile (.8 km) away. In the state of Iowa, officials tested air quality in six different neighborhoods adjacent to hog farms. Data collected showed hydrogen sulfide and ammonia levels frequently exceeded the state's recommended air quality levels. It is believed that these elevated levels have led to numerous adverse health effects, including headaches, asthma, flu-like symptoms, and diarrhea.

"The coincidence of people showing a pattern of impairment and being exposed to hydrogen sulfide arising from lagoons where hog manure is stored and then sprayed on fields or sprayed into the air demonstrates a link that is practically undeniable," says Kaye Kilburn, MD, a professor of medicine at the University of Southern California.

According to the FAO, animal agriculture is responsible for 18 percent of all greenhouse gas emissions. Annually, animals raised for food account for 9 percent of carbon dioxide, 37 percent of methane, and 65 percent of nitrous oxide.

Depleting fossil fuels: In addition to water, soil, and air pollution, the effect of animal agriculture has on fossil fuels is tremendous. Each animal grown and slaughtered for food must be fed. The feed ranges from grain to soy products. This feed requires energy to grow and transport. During 2012, China imported around 60 percent of the world's total soybean produced, primarily to feed pigs. Just imagine the amount of people that could be fed if we focused our agriculture on wheat, corn, soy, and other grains grown for human consumption rather than for livestock.

Concentrated Animal Feeding Operations

A Concentrated Animal Feeding Operation (CAFO) is a factory farm that houses hundreds, even thousands, of animals in a small concentrated area. The effect CAFOs have on the environment is stifling. Because these large commercial operations are still considered farms, they are exempt from the emission standards for other types of industrial operations. Factory farms do not have to follow the same rules when it comes to disposing of waste and emitting harmful greenhouse gasses and other highly toxic pollutants that other types of factories do. Because of this loophole, CAFOs contribute about 80 percent of the ammonia emissions.

The fecal waste from these large operations is more than 100 times that of all of the U.S. human population combined. Yes, you read that right. The fecal waste from CAFOs is more than 100 times the waste of more than 313 million people! Human waste, however, is treated in sewer systems. Not so with agricultural animal waste. This waste finds its way into the groundwater and eventually into our rivers and oceans. The EPA found that waste from factory farms has already contaminated the groundwater in 17 states and polluted more than 35,000 miles (56,000 km) of rivers in 22 states.

The waste from these CAFOs polluting the waterways with, well, let's be blunt, pee and poop. That pee and poop is also filled with the antibiotics and hormones that are fed to these animals. Tests have shown that these secreted drugs affect our food supply. Vegetables grown on farms adjacent to CAFOs have been shown to contain low doses of hormones and antibiotics. Fish that swim in polluted waterways have also tested positive for these harmful drugs.

Fish and Seafood

Our oceans are very fragile, and as humans' appetite for seafood grows, the havoc it is wreaking on the oceans grows. In fact, it is already driving many species to extinction. If overfishing trends continue, the FAO estimates that all wild fish may be gone by the year 2048.

For every pound (455 g) of shrimp that makes it to the plate, up to 20 pounds (9 kg) of other marine life is caught, killed or maimed, and discarded. Each year, hundreds of thousands of what the industry calls "by-catch," are caught or tangled up in nets and then thrown back into the ocean. The victims include dolphins, turtles, and other marine animals.

Farmed fish (aquaculture) isn't any better. Many fisheries use wild fish as feed for farmed fish, sometimes using up to 5 pounds (2.25 kg) of wild caught fish to grow just 1 pound (455 g) of farm raised fish.

Out of greed, and to make maximum profits, commercial fish farms overcrowd their fish. This overcrowding breeds disease and causes stress for the fish. Studies have shown that too dense a stocking rate induces stress problems and increases susceptibility to diseases. Overcrowding also leads to poor water quality due to decreased oxygen levels, high accumulation of metabolic products and excrement, and rapid growth and transmission of noxious parasites, microorganisms, and pathogens.

Make the World a Greener Place. Go Vegan!

A report in *New Scientist* estimated that driving a hybrid car rather than an average vehicle conserves a little over 1 ton (907 kg) of carbon dioxide per year. And a report from *Shrink that Footprint,* which compares the carbon footprints of five different diets, shows that a vegan diet, consumes about 1½ tons (1360 kg) less than the Sickness and Disease-promoting diet. Adopting a plant-based diet actually does more to reduce emissions than driving a hybrid car!

Many scientists and environmentalists agree that adopting a plant-based diet is surely a step in the right direction to ensuring a reduction in greenhouse gas emissions and a reduction in the overall waste of energy in food production.

Years ago, as big business began operating CAFOs and other large-scale factory farms, it was with the promise that food would be cheaper and healthier. They promised it would make it possible to reduce hunger throughout the world. Unfortunately, we now know this couldn't be farther from the truth. Instead, the larger the farm, the bigger its negative impact is on the environment. And because so much of the farmland is being used to grow livestock feed, instead of food for human consumption, the problem of world hunger has only increased.

We urge you to stop supporting animal agriculture with your consumer dollar. Whenever possible, purchase local, seasonal, and organically grown produce. This will ensure that you are reducing your food's carbon footprint even further.

Chapter 3

Do It for Your Wallet!

One of the scariest parts of going vegan is the fear that it might be expensive. But that simply isn't the case. Sure, if you pack your cart full of processed mockmeats and cheeses every trip to the grocery store, you probably won't be saving any money. But going vegan doesn't have to mean going broke.

In this chapter, we will compare the costs of an animal-based diet and a plant-based one. We'll show you how to save money by skipping the highly processed faux foods and shopping for "ingredients" rather than for "food." We will also discuss the importance of shopping the perimeter of the grocery store, using the local farmers' markets, and growing your own gardens to save extra money. We will talk about how adopting a plant-based lifestyle will save you money in the checkout line, and it will also save you money on your health care bills.

Reduce Your Grocery Bill—Go Vegan!

Probably the best way to save money by going vegan is to grow your own food. You can also save money by joining a co-op, community-supported agriculture (CSA), or shopping at a farmers' market. But we understand that those options don't work for everyone.

The good news is that even when shopping at a grocery store, switching to a plant-based diet will save you money. We're always amazed when people try to tell us that eating healthfully is more expensive. Let's look at the type of food you would eat on a plant-based diet and compare that with the food a person eats on a Sickness and Disease-promoting Diet.

For a plant-based lifestyle, the main staples that you would purchase are beans, leafy greens, vegetables, rice, potatoes or sweet potatoes, grains, fruits, and nuts/seeds. We recommend that you purchase as much as you can in bulk and start cooking the basic components of your meals in batches. One of Gerrie's favorite mottoes is "Cook once and eat three or four times." The more you can cook in larger batches and store in containers to be frozen or used during the week, the easier a plant-based lifestyle becomes.

The bulk section in your grocery store offers the least expensive way to purchase your food, because packaging is the most expensive part of any product. For the type of foods that you will be eating, the product will cost just pennies, but the packaging will cost dollars.

Reduce Your Health Care Bill—Go Vegan!

Hopefully we've convinced you that going vegan will save you money on food costs. It will also save you money on health care. Here's why.

When you calculate the cost to your health caused by the Sickness and Disease-promoting Diet (aptly abbreviated as SAD!), there is no comparison. It may be easier to drive through a fast-food restaurant to purchase your burger, but you'd better add the cost of insulin for type 2 diabetes, blood pressure medication, or worse yet, for heart bypass surgery or the hospitalization costs for a heart attack or stroke. Facts have shown that it is just a matter of time before you suffer some type of Western disease when you indulge in a diet filled with overprocessed foods that are lacking in fiber, vitamins, minerals, and phytochemicals.

THREE SIMPLE TRICKS FOR SAVING AT THE SUPERMARKET

Shop the perimeter of the store. By spending the majority of your shopping trip in the perimeter of the store, you'll avoid the most expensive packaged and processed foods. Around the store's perimeter, you'll find the fresh produce, bulk bins, tofu, tempeh, nondairy milks and yogurts, and other fresh ingredients.

Buy in bulk. As stated previously, buying in bulk is far cheaper than buying foods in packages. From simple staples such as rice and beans to specialty ingredients such as nutritional yeast, textured vegetable protein, spices, and more, buying in bulk is one of the single biggest money-savers in the supermarket. Plus it's better for the environment, too!

Buy local and in season. We're now almost hardwired to believe that all produce grows year round. Sure, in today's global market, we're able to get fresh oranges in July and fresh peaches in December, but the truth is that these items are shipped in from places around the world where they are in season, or they are grown in specialty greenhouses that increase the cost significantly.

Local growers have seasonal produce in abundance, and that produce is far cheaper than produce that has to be shipped from halfway around the world.

In addition, there's a reason there's a season. Fruits and vegetables are more flavorful and more nutrient-dense when grown and consumed in their rightful seasons. We have all experienced eating a fruit or vegetable out of season and saying, "This just isn't very flavorful."

Save by Growing Your Own Food

Obviously, not everyone has the luxury of living on a few acres out in the country where you can have your own organic garden year round. Most of us are lucky to even have a window where we can grow a few pots of herbs! But that's okay. Fresh herbs are sometimes all it takes to turn a bland, boring meal into a culinary masterpiece that would have cost way more had it been purchased in a restaurant. Here are some tips for growing your own food at home, whether in an apartment, a house, or on a farmstead.

Start with organic seeds. They will be clearly marked and are readily available at nurseries, garden centers, and health food stores or through online sources. By starting out with seeds that are free from genetic manipulation, you are ensuring your crop is off to a good start. If you are a bit impatient, you can also start out with organic living plants.

Many food plants are available for purchase. Herbs are a great example of this. Some supermarkets sell basil, cilantro, rosemary, and other herbs already fully mature in pots ready for use in your culinary creations. You can transplant these mini plants into larger, more practical containers for the home. (This is how Joni rolls when it comes to her home gardening.)

Know your zone. If you're growing outdoors, research your plant hardiness zones. Most plants and seeds list what zones and time of year in which the plant will thrive. By knowing these facts up front and choosing appropriate plants and seeds for your zone, you'll set yourself up for success.

Plant in pots. If you have limited space (or even if you don't!), planting in pots makes growing your food much more manageable. In addition, growing in pots helps keep weeds at bay. It also allows you to move your plants should you need to.

Go vertical. Vertical gardening is a great way to grow in a small space, even indoors! Using hydroponic (water-only, no soil) techniques, a vertical garden tower is a great way to grow a potted garden in a small space with minimal mess and an easy watering system. If you have a little extra space to spare, you can grow towers full of plants designated for different uses. Only your imagination can set the limits on configuration—a salsa garden, a salad garden, an herb garden.

Have a plan for care. Growing your own food takes time and patience. Schedule time to tend to your plants. Use this time as a getaway from the hustle and bustle of everyday life, and as a time to connect with your food.

Think of each meal you eat that uses something you've grown yourself as a reward for your hard work and dedication to your well-being!

Save by Shopping at Co-ops, CSAs, and Farmers' Markets

Almost every community has a co-op, a CSA, or a farmers' market. If you're lucky, your community may have all three! Each and every one of these options is a great way to spend less on your grocery bill and have the chance to enjoy seasonal fresh fruit and veggies at their peak. Let's talk about each in turn.

CO-OPS

A food co-op (short for cooperative) is a collectively owned grocery store. It usually focuses on making natural foods more affordable for members. Communities of all sizes have food co-ops, ranging from very small to quite large. Most commonly, there are two types of co-op, private and public. Both of them share the common values of group management and decision-making, social responsibility, and equality.

In a private food co-op, only members may shop at the store. To become a member, you pay a small initiation fee and usually invest a set amount of money in the organization to purchase a share. Some co-ops allow members to purchase multiple shares, or require an annual fee, which causes long-term members to own more shares. In some cases, members also join work crews, contributing a few hours of work to the running of the co-op. The frequency and duration of work shifts varies from co-op to co-op.

In a public food co-op, anyone may shop at the store, but only members receive special discounted prices. Anyone may join the co-op. The prices for non-members in this type of store are often lower than at other retail stores to encourage people to shop at the co-op even if they cannot join. To find a co-op near you, visit www.coopdirectory.org

COMMUNITY-SUPPORTED AGRICULTURE

Community-supported agriculture (CSA) is a system in which you can "share" in a farm. In return, you receive a weekly, bi-weekly, or monthly box of fresh produce. These boxes might be delivered directly to your door, or you might pick them up at points throughout the community. CSAs do not really allow you to choose what produce you will receive; rather you're given a variety of what's in season. The prices can vary, but they are generally far lower than that of any grocery store.

Some advantages of joining a CSA include the opportunity to eat fresh, local food, full of flavor and nutrition; getting exposed to new vegetables and new ways of cooking; getting to visit the farm where the food is grown; developing a relationship with the farmer who grows your food; and learning more about how food is grown.

To find a CSA near you, visit LocalHarvest.org and enter your zip code into the search function. You'll be connected with one of more than 4,000 CSAs registered throughout the country.

FARMERS' MARKETS

A farmers' market is another way to meet and get to know the people growing your food, all while saving money on the freshest seasonal local produce. Local farmers, bakers, and other artisans and entrepreneurs get together in a public place—usually a parking lot, park, or along the sidewalk—and provide their wares to the local community for a discounted price. Many communities host at least one farmers' market every week.

Some produce at farmers' markets will be certified organic. Other times, farmers use organic practices when growing, but because of the time and money needed to get certified as organic, they are unable to label their produce as such, therefore making organic produce far more affordable. How can you find out how a crop is grown? Simply ask the farmer at the market! By going to farmers' markets and talking directly with the farmers, you can find out how your food is grown, and you can support local farmers and business at the same time. To find a local farmers' market near you, visit FarmersMarket.com and enter your zip code.

So far we've shown you that adopting a well-balanced plant-based diet is better for your health and the environment, and for your wallet, too. Continue on to read how it also helps the animals.

ANDREA CRAWFORD, FOUNDER AND FARMER AT KENTER CANYON FARMS

Joni was lucky enough to meet Andrea on a tour of one of her ranches in Ventura County, California. She was a gracious host and tour guide. She told of the land's history, and the passion in her voice was evidence that she really cares about what she does. As we walked through the fields admiring the organic herbs and baby greens (and often picking a few to eat!), she shared her story.

Andrea was a landscape painter and lived on a boat moored in the Berkeley Marina with her then-husband, Dennis Peitso. She wanted to grow herbs and lettuces to paint. Back then, you were lucky to find fresh cilantro and parsley, let alone other fresh herbs, frisse, baby arugula, mesclun, or even kale, at the local grocer. She also worked at a restaurant called Chez Panisse, which was owned by Alice Water.

Andrea didn't have her own yard in which to garden, so Alice allowed Andrea to use hers. And garden she did. Andrea wondered what she would do with all of the lettuces she grew and couldn't use herself. So, Alice used the lettuces in her restaurant.

In 1981, Andrea had a newborn son, and she wondered what she was going to do to make a living. Alice sparked Andrea's entrepreneurial spirit by offering to pay Andrea for her lettuces. So Andrea's garden grew. And word started to get around. Soon, Andrea got a call from Wolfgang Puck, offering to pay for space for Andrea to grow and supply lettuces and fresh herbs for his new restaurant, Spago, in Los Angeles.

With a shorter growing season in Berkeley than in sunny southern California, and an offer that seemed too good to be true, in 1985 Andrea and Dennis decided to moor their boat in Marina Del Rey and give the LA farming scene a go.

Andrea and Dennis planted their first garden in the backyard of Puck's pastry chef's father in Encino. But more space was needed, so they became urban farmers and leased some ground space under the electrical wires in Tarzana and Agoura Hills. Andrea began growing more, selling the lettuces at local farmers' markets and, of course, to Wolfgang Puck.

Andrea's farm needed a name, and it was serendipitous. The power lines overhead were the DWP Kenter Canyon Power Lines, so she named her farm Kenter Canyon Farms.

Longer growing seasons and more space allowed the business to grow. In 1988, Andrea and Dennis amicably divorced and split the company. Dennis kept the Agoura Hills and Tarzana farms and renamed them Maggie's Farms, while Andrea moved Kenter Canyon Farms to Filmore. That's where Andrea, now remarried, runs the organic farm that Joni was lucky enough to tour.

"Kenter Canyon Farms is a family farm located in Ventura County, growing lettuces, herbs, and specialty crops year-round in the fertile soil along the Santa Clara River," Andrea says. "Our produce is harvested daily, washed and packed in our own certified facility, and distributed every day to local customers, including farmers' markets, restaurants, hotels, produce purveyors, and retail stores. Our dedication is to quality and freshness and to growing produce that we ourselves wish to eat every day. We are committed to sustainable agricultural practices and to our employees who sustain our farm year-round."

Humble beginnings have led to a life-changing career path. From a shared backyard garden to a sustainable organic farm! Now, after more than thirty years in the farming business, Andrea owns and operates many ranches throughout California with her husband that focus on local distribution, all sharing the same mission of sustainability.

After the tour, Joni was treated to a farm-fresh lunch that included a variety of herbs and greens grown on the farm and prepared in a delicious salad, an amazing Kenter Canyon Farms Greens Goddess Dressing (see the recipe on page 140) made with herbs grown on the farm, and artisan loaves of freshly baked bread made with flour milled with the three varieties of heritage wheat grown on the farm. "I have never had such an amazing meal. Talk about connecting with your food," says Joni.

Chapter 4

Do It for the Animals!

We humans sure do have an ego! This chapter will delve into the horrors of animal cruelty as it exists in the world of animal agriculture, and how raising animals for food has led to uncountable atrocities both against the animals and the humans who work in these extreme conditions.

The invention of refrigeration led to insurmountable growth in the meat and poultry industry. With refrigeration, an animal can be slaughtered, eviscerated, and aseptically packaged, not even resembling the animal it came from, and shipped all the way across the country, and in some cases the world, to a supermarket near you.. This creates a complete disconnect, and therefore disrespect, for the animal that gave its life unwillingly for food.

In this chapter, we'll talk about how going vegan will help you to help animals. We'll talk about the evils of speciesism and "humane" meat. We'll also explain how chickens, cows, and pigs are treated in factories.

Speciesism

"We should always be clear that animal exploitation is wrong because it involves speciesism. And speciesism is wrong because, like racism, sexism, homophobia, anti-Semitism, classism, and all other forms of human discrimination, speciesism involves violence inflicted on members of the moral community where that infliction of violence cannot be morally justified." — Gary L. Francione, legal scholar and pioneer of the Abolitionist Theory of animal rights.

Speciesism is probably best described as human superiorism. Like a racist, a speciesist is someone who believes that humans are far superior to all other species and that all non-human animals should not be afforded the same protections that are afforded to humans. This way of thinking allows human animals to abuse and exploit non-human animals for food, clothing, and entertainment.

"Humane" Meat

Have you ever heard this term? Humane meat is defined as meat that was raised in a humane and compassionate way. In other words, the farmer who raised the animals raised them in a way that was compassionate prior to sending that animal to slaughter. This term is an advertising buzzword, designed to make people feel better about the animal foods they are purchasing, as if for some reason raising the animal in a more humane way makes it okay to kill it for food later in life. The term itself is an oxymoron. Regardless of how an animal is treated throughout its life, the end result is the same. Death for dollars. Whether it is a free-range chicken or a grass-fed cow (and we will get to those terms shortly), the sad truth is that these animals that are raised for food will all end up the same. Dead. It's a sad reality that 99 percent of all animals raised for food are raised on factory farms. Chickens, beef cattle, and pigs are all subjected to atrocities in these farms.

CHICKENS

Did you know that chickens are quite intelligent? Studies show they have the intelligence equal to most dogs and cats—even some primates. Chickens are quite social as well, and they enjoy living in groups. They find their place in the pecking order and enjoy taking dust baths and basking in the sun. Chickens raised for poultry and egg-laying hens, however, are now completely different breeds. Both suffer terrible, brief lives.

Chickens Raised for Their Meat

Of all animals raised for food, chickens probably have it the worst. Worldwide, more than 50 billion chickens are slaughtered each year for food. That is 95,129 chickens slaughtered for every single minute of every single hour of every single day.

From the minute they hatch, factory farm–raised chickens spend their lives in confinement. Once hatched in a commercial hatchery, the chicks are sprayed with vaccines and packed into crates to be shipped to the "farm." Once they arrive at a rearing shed, they will stay there until they are shipped off to slaughter.

These chickens are bred and injected with antibiotics and growth hormones to grow so quickly their organs often fail. Heart attacks are common, especially under the extreme stress and conditions in a broiler shed.

Even so-called cage-free or free-range chickens are kept in warehouses that are known as broiler sheds. For a chicken to be called cage-free or free-range, it has to have a door to allow for outdoor access. No rules govern how often those birds get to experience the outside, or how big that outdoor space needs to be. Some free-range broiler sheds have an outdoor space of only about 5 feet by 5 feet (1.52 sq m) for thousands of birds.

Tens of thousands of chicks are packed into these sheds. As the chickens grow, the space gets tighter. Because the chickens are bred for big breasts—the most desirable part of a chicken—they often have a hard time walking. Their legs are not strong enough to hold them up. The chickens fall down, get trampled on by the other chickens, and die. That is commonplace in the industry.

During the chickens' time in the shed, the litter is never changed. It gets pretty smelly in those sheds. The soiled litter burns the legs and bellies of the chickens.

When the chickens are only six to seven weeks old, it's time to go to slaughter. The farm workers come to collect all of the birds at once, often grabbing them by the ankles and violently throwing them into crates. They then stack the crates onto trucks and send them to the slaughterhouses.

At the slaughterhouse, the chickens are shackled by their ankles and hung upside down on conveyors that run their heads into a "stunning" water bath, where they're electrocuted until they're unconscious. Their throats are then slit. Often chickens, being the intelligent creatures that they are, will raise their heads to avoid the stunning water bath, and the chickens then have their throats slit while fully conscious.

After the farmers have removed the chickens from the barn, plenty of dead birds remain on the broiler shed floor. The house is cleaned out, and the whole process starts over.

Chickens Raised for Their Eggs

Whether sourced from a factory farm or a free-range ranch, the truth is, eggs are not all they are cracked up to be, even if sourced from your own backyard.

The idealistic farm with the big red barn, the farmer working the fields, and the farmer's wife feeding the chickens and collecting the eggs to sell to the neighborhood market has become all but extinct. They have been replaced by large corporate factory farms. The more chickens that can fit into the smallest possible space mean more eggs and more profits. Unfortunately, this leads to the decline in quality of life of those poor egg-laying chickens.

But eating their eggs doesn't hurt the chicken, right? Wrong. Egg-laying hens lead some of the most cruelty-filled lives of all animals bred for food. From the moment they hatch, the suffering begins. Virtually all egg-laying hens come from hatcheries that kill all male chicks shortly after hatching. Because the males are of no use to the egg industry, since they don't lay eggs and aren't bred to grow as large or as rapidly as chickens used in the meat industry, they are quickly sorted out and suffocated, gassed, or thrown into a grinder, while still alive.

Things aren't much better for the females. Once sorted from the male chicks, females are often packed into shipping boxes and shipped off to fill orders. When they arrive at the rearing facility, they are either placed in cages or sheds, depending on which type of facility they are at, and raised until they reach egg-laying age, or about seventeen weeks old. At the rearing facility, they get exposed to increasing lengths of light in the sheds. By altering the levels of light, the sleep levels and behaviors of the hens are affected, which stimulates their ability to produce eggs.

Once the chickens reach egg-producing age, they are transferred to an egg-laying facility. The hens will become a part of the system, whether it is a battery cage, a cage-free warehouse, or a free-range facility. The majority of the hens' short lives are spent here.

Regardless of the facility, many of the same practices occur. Debeaking is a common practice in which the beaks of the birds are seared off with a hot blade to prevent the birds from pecking at each other. Why? Because thousands of birds can be held in just one warehouse, and even without cages, these birds are kept so closely together that they don't always get along. Imagine being stuck in an elevator with twenty other adults for one-and-a-half years—the average lifespan of an egg-laying hen. You'd be pecking at each other, too!

The natural lifespan of a chicken can be up to twelve years, but due to the strain and breeding of today's egg-laying hen, that is commonly reduced to about seventy-two weeks. When the hen reaches about seventy-two weeks old, her egg production decreases, making her less profitable. Some egg producers then put the chickens through the horrific process of forced molting, which can re-invigorate egg production. Forced molting occurs when feed is withheld or severely reduced for up to two weeks, causing a marked reduction in body weight.

Once chickens stop laying "enough" eggs, they are considered spent. Spent chickens are rounded up and packed into crates where they are marked for slaughter. Because egg-laying hens are a different breed than those raised for meat, and also because their bodies are too bruised and beaten, they are either ground up to be used as fertilizer, or they are processed into low-quality products, such as soups and stocks, and animal food, such as dog or cat food.

What about backyard eggs? While it is true that the quality of the lives of most backyard chickens are leaps and bounds ahead of those raised on commercial factory farms, there are still a couple of reasons why backyard eggs should not be eaten. Just like those in factory farms, most backyard chickens come from hatcheries. And ordering up a box of egg-laying hens directly contributes to the death and suffering of hundreds of millions of male chicks each and every year.

Besides, the eggs don't belong to you. Did you know it takes a hen about twenty-five hours to produce just one egg? The amount of energy and resources it takes for her to produce that egg takes a lot out of her. And if left to her own devices, once she realizes the egg is not fertilized, she might even crack the egg open and eat it, shell and all, to regain those nutrients.

MEET TURKEY LURKEY

Each year, hundreds of millions of turkeys are slaughtered, 45 million for Thanksgiving alone. Poultry animals are explicitly excluded from the federal Humane Slaughter Act, and so they are not required to be rendered unconscious before they are killed. Countless turkeys die terrified and in pain in grisly slaughterhouses.

Turkey Lurkey was brought to Farm Sanctuary by a woman who had rescued her from a farm, saving the friendly bird from becoming a holiday meal. Safe forever from that fate, Turkey Lurkey now receives only kindness from humans, and she adores them in return. This sweet turkey follows guests around like a dog. She loves it when they pet her gently on the head and scratch her chest.

COWS

Like chickens, cows are subjected to cruel situations on factory farms and ranches.

Cows Raised for Beef

These animals probably have it better than any other animal raised for food, but that's not saying much. Many beef cattle are born and live on a range, for months or sometimes even years. Calves are able to feed from their mothers, and social behaviors are formed.

However, cattle are not adequately protected against extreme cold or extreme hot weather. They may die of dehydration or freeze to death. When the animals are injured or sick, they don't always receive the necessary veterinary attention. On the ranch, the following extremely inhumane practices occur.

* **Castration:** Male calves' testicles are ripped from their scrotums, often without anesthesia.

* **Branding:** Ranchers brand cattle with hot iron brands to identify them. This practice is extremely traumatic and painful, and it's done without anesthesia. Branding causes third-degree burns, and the cows bellow in pain and attempt to escape.

* **Waddling:** Beef cattle are also subjected to waddling, which is another type of identification marking. This painful procedure entails cutting chunks out of the hide that hangs under the animals' necks. Waddling marks are supposed to be large enough so that ranchers can identify their cattle from a distance.

After months or even years on the range, cattle are frightened and confused when people come to round them up. Terrified animals are often injured, some so severely that they become "downed" and are unable to walk or even stand. These downed animals commonly suffer for days without receiving food, water, or veterinary care. Many die of neglect. Other downed animals are dragged or pushed with tractors on their way to the stockyards.

Once at the stockyards, cattle are further frightened and confused as they're forced through a series of walkways and holding pens. Then they are shown to and sold to the highest bidder.

Upon reaching maturity, cattle are trucked to a feedlot to be fattened up and readied for slaughter. At feedlots, cattle are crowded by the thousands into dry, dusty, manure-filled holding pens. The odor in the air can be smelled for miles, and it's full of harmful bacteria, ammonia, methane, and other noxious chemicals, subjecting the cattle to a constant risk of respiratory infection. Cattle on feedlots are fed a highly unnatural diet to fatten them up. They're routinely implanted with growth hormones and antibiotics.

Eventually, all cattle will go to a slaughterhouse, and that last trip can be a terrible one. Cattle do not travel well, and the stress of being confined in shipping trailers causes immense stress to the animals. Ironically, many animals are injured or die on the way to be killed.

A standard beef slaughterhouse kills 250 cattle every hour—four every minute.

MEET PINTO

When Pinto was found during an investigation of a California "calf ranch," he was confined to a crate and too weak to stand. Over the years, we have encountered many such ailing calves.

Male calves are a byproduct of the dairy industry, which must breed cows to keep them in milk production, but has no use for the males whose births inevitably result. The male calves are taken from their mothers as newborns and sold to be raised for cheap beef or veal, often in deplorable conditions.

Dead and dying calves are a common sight at calf ranches. Pinto, however, lived to know a better fate. Once his release was secured, he was rushed to safety. With emergency veterinary treatment and lots of TLC, he made a full recovery.

This carefree, young, 3,000-pound (1360 kg) steer is now safe at Animal Acres, Farm Sanctuary's Southern California shelter, playing, grazing, and soaking up the good life.

Prior to being hung up by their back legs and bled to death, cattle are supposed to be rendered unconscious. This stunning is usually done by a mechanical blow to the head. However, the procedure is terribly imprecise, and inadequate stunning is inevitable. As a result, conscious animals are often hung upside down, kicking and struggling, while a slaughterhouse worker makes another attempt to render them unconscious. Eventually, the animals' throats will be sliced, whether or not they are unconscious.

Calves raised for veal live their entire lives in wooden crates tethered by their necks without room to walk, turn around, or even just lie down. Calves raised to become veal are also purposely fed an all-liquid milk substitute that is deficient in iron and fiber in order to produce anemia, which results in the pale-colored flesh typical of veal. Veal calves are slaughtered at the ripe old age of four to five months old, and they are unable to walk to slaughter because their muscles are severely underdeveloped. Some veal calves are killed at just a few days old to be sold as low-grade "bob" veal for products such as frozen TV dinners.

Cows Raised for Their Milk

What about dairy cows? They don't get killed for the milk. Many people consume dairy products, even if they've given up meat, because they don't think that taking milk from the cow hurts the cow. And while it may be true that a dairy cow is not killed for her milk, the real truth is that a cow doesn't produce milk if it isn't giving birth to a calf.

Dairy cows are kept pregnant constantly, and once those cows give birth, the calves are almost immediately whisked away from their mothers. In most commercial dairy operations, this means that the girls are kept and raised to live out the same fate as their mothers, and the boys are either sent off to auction to the veal industry, or they are just simply left to die.

If we were able to read the mind of a dairy cow, she would tell us she would rather be killed than endure being constantly pregnant, only to have her calves stolen from her at birth. She would tell how she is constantly strapped to a painful milking machine that causes her udders to chafe and get infected with puss-filled sores.

A domestic cow has a lifespan of up to twenty years, but the average dairy cow very rarely lives past the age of four. Cows raised for milk production are generally removed from the herd at age four and sold for beef. Almost 20 percent of the beef produced in the United States comes from "spent" dairy cows. In other words, if the cow is not producing at least 3 to 4 gallons (12 to 15 liters) of milk per day, it is not commercially viable to keep her around. So she is sent to slaughter.

PIGS

Pigs are very smart animals. Studies have shown that they are as smart as a three-year-old child. The poor piggy really gets a bad rap as a dirty and messy animal. The truth is, these sweet hogs only wallow in the mud as a way to cool off and protect themselves from the sun. Did you know that pigs can't sweat? The saying, "Sweat like a pig," actually makes no sense at all! In fact, pigs are some of the cleanest animals. They make a conscious effort not to ever defecate where they eat or sleep.

Pigs are natural problem solvers. They are even more trainable than dogs and cats.

Did we mention these sweeties are actually naturally lean as well? Yep, they only get fat when they have been overfed by humans.

The pork industry is simply disgusting. Many large factory pig farms house their pigs in deplorable conditions. Many are kept in gestation crates. That's a metal enclosure where a sow is kept during pregnancy—and most of her adult life.

The enclosures measure 6.6 × 2 feet (2 m × 60 cm) and house sows that weigh up to 600 pounds (270 kg). The floors of the crates are made of cold, hard concrete, and they're slotted so that her waste can be collected below. Remember that pigs do not like to defecate where they sleep or eat, so this causes immense stress to her.

As the pig outgrows the crate, she is forced to sleep on her chest, unable to even turn around. A few days before giving birth, she will be moved to a farrowing crate, where she is able to lie down to nurse. Though that's the only time she sees her piglets. Otherwise, they are housed apart from her.

This practice is physically abhorable, and the practice is emotional torture for the animal. The pig is constantly kept in a crate, unable to even turn around, let alone get comfortable, only to have her babies kept separated from her as she nurses. The pig lies on her side, so her nipples are available to the piglets for nursing; the piglets are kept in an adjacent pen, separated by a fence or bars, where mama cannot even cuddle and coo her babies. The babies are eventually taken away completely only to have the entire process repeated over and over again.

Pork producers argue that gestation crates are needed because sows housed so closely together will fight, but a trip to a farm sanctuary will show that 600-pound (272 kg) pigs indeed live in harmony together without the use of cages. In fact, they create their own hierarchy among themselves. When a group of unacquainted pigs are first placed together, they will fight to establish a dominance hierarchy. The fighting behavior is generally mouth-to-neck attacks with strong thrusts sideways and upwards. After about an hour, the level of aggression drops dramatically. Within twenty-four hours of mixing, the hierarchy will be established.

Piglets are stolen away from their mothers at just a few weeks old. Their tails are chopped off, the ends of their teeth are snipped off with pliers, and the males are castrated—all without anesthesia. The pigs then spend their entire lives in extremely crowded pens on tiny slabs of filthy concrete. Pig farms are some of the saddest places on earth. Confined pigs cry and bite at the bars of their tiny pens out of boredom.

Pigs naturally live for ten to fifteen years. But factory-farmed pigs are sent to slaughter after just six months. The pigs are forced onto transport trucks that travel for many miles through all sorts of weather extremes to take them to the slaughterhouse. Many die of heat exhaustion in the summer or freeze to death in the winter.

A typical slaughterhouse kills up to 1,000 pigs an hour—sixteen per minute. Because of improper stunning methods, many pigs are still fully awake, conscious, and squealing when they are dumped into scalding-hot water, which is intended to remove their hair and soften their skin.

End the Suffering

You picked up this book for a reason. You read this chapter because deep down you knew that giving up meat and adopting a cruelty-free way of life was the right thing to do. Ignore the naysayers who tell you that one person won't make a difference, because they're wrong. On average, each meat-eating person contributes to the death of more than 100 animals each year. So if you think you, just one person, won't make a difference, we can assure you that those 100 animals certainly disagree. So stop the suffering and become a WellBeing.

MEET SOPHIE

Sophie was rescued from a Future Farmers of America (FFA) project, and what she experienced as its subject hardly inspires confidence in the future of American farming. Young people who participate in FFA are each expected to raise a farm animal of their choice and then auction him or her for slaughter at the local fair. As they awaited this doom, Sophie and her fellow FFA pigs lived in a small concrete pen without bedding or comfort of any kind. Most developed sores, and all were constantly harassed by flies. The pigs had also been subjected to ear-notching, which is a common industry procedure in which pieces of the ear are cut out, without anesthetic, for identification.

This grim life did not, however, come to a grim end for Sophie and her best friend, Alicia. Disillusioned with the project, the young woman responsible for the two pigs decided to find a home for them instead. Now Sophie and Alicia are safe at Farm Sanctuary's Southern California Shelter, where they teach visitors lessons in compassion, ensuring that the future of farm animals in America will be brighter.

Chapter 5

Stocking a Vegan Kitchen

In this chapter, we will teach you how to shop. We'll navigate the supermarket aisles right alongside you, teaching you how to read and decipher the ingredients listed on labels and showing you how you can make easy, simple swaps to replace animal-based products with vegan versions of the same thing! We'll guide you through stocking your vegan kitchen and teach you about some of those "weird" vegan ingredients.

Know What's Going in Your Cart

In addition to knowing what individual ingredients you should avoid in packaged food to achieve a plant-based diet, we also want to give you some rules for making sure that any vegan product you choose is also promoting good health.

None of us, other than infants, would just put something into our mouths without knowing what it is and if it is good for us. Yet, every day, most of us walk into a grocery store and make the assumption that because it is on the shelf, it is good for us. Never make that mistake! We know the thought of reading labels on packaged products that you buy seems like a terrible inconvenience to many people, but we promise you'll be amazed at what you see in some of your favorite products. It doesn't take very long before you won't have to look at labels because you'll get a good feel for which products are more likely to have ingredients or levels of fats, sodium, and sugars that we just don't want in our food. Here are two simple rules.

Never, ever, never believe the statements made on the front of packages. Statements such as "low in sodium," "lightly salted," and "lower in fats" sound good, but what do they really mean? Lower in sodium than what? What amount of salt does a lightly salted product contain? Food marketers know what buzzwords consumers are looking for in healthier foods. They manipulate their message so it's not legally incorrect; however, it still misleads consumers into believing it is healthy.

Read the nutrition panel. While ignoring the claims on the front of the package, simply turn the package over and look at the back. Here's what you want to look for.

SERVING SIZE

First of all, look at the serving size. Remember that the numbers on a nutrition label are representative of *one serving*. Food manufacturers manipulate the serving size. They generally use a serving size that is unrealistically small so that the numbers on the nutrition label will please the consumer. For example, if the package says that there are 300 calories per serving, but there are two servings in the package, and you eat the whole package, then you have eaten 600 calories.

Here's an example. Spray oils are one product where they really manipulate the numbers on a nutrition facts panel. The spray oils we use to spray on our pans when cooking are 100 percent oil in the can, but the label reads "fat free." How can that be when all oils are 100 percent calories from fat? The answer is that the manufacturer uses a serving size that results in 0.5 grams of fat. The government rule is that when a serving size has 0.5 grams of any nutrient, it can be rounded down to zero. So the manufacturer uses a serving size that results in 0.25 grams of fat, which for a spray cooking oil is a serving size that comes out of the can in $\frac{1}{120}$th of a second! What in the world is $\frac{1}{120}$th of a second? One little spritz takes almost 1 second. But if you read "fat free" on the label, you might think that there is no fat in the can and liberally spray the oil all over your food, resulting in hundreds of empty calories! So watch that serving size.

FAT

The next number you should look at is the amount of fat in the product. In addition to the total fat, two types of fat are specifically listed on a nutrition facts panel: saturated fat and trans fat. Let's talk about each.

Saturated fat: It's recommended that we get 7 percent or less of our daily calories from saturated fats. So the amount of saturated fat in a product should be very low—preferably zero. You should also do a quick mathematical calculation on the number of calories from fat. If you are eating for your health, and more than 40 percent of the calories are from fat, put the product back on the shelf, even if those calories are coming from "good" fats, such as mono- or polyunsaturated fats.

Trans fats: The government has suggested that we avoid getting any trans fats in our diet at all. So trans fats should always read zero.

When you add together the total saturated fat and the trans fat and subtract that from the total fat, what you have left is the "good" fat.

CHOLESTEROL

Cholesterol is another number to look out for on the nutrition label. Our bodies make all the cholesterol we need, so we should not eat products that contribute any cholesterol. The amount of cholesterol in a food you eat should always be zero. Luckily for us, all plant-based food is cholesterol-free. If you see cholesterol on the label, put the product back on the shelf. The product is not vegan.

SODIUM

Sodium, i.e. salt, is another important number to look out for in packaged foods. A real easy rule to follow for sodium is that there should be no greater than a 1:1 ratio of milligrams of sodium to calories per serving. So if there are 110 calories per serving, there should be no more than 110 milligrams of sodium in that serving. If that number goes slightly over, it isn't a big deal, but try to stick as close to the 1:1 ratio as possible.

CARBOHYDRATES

The preferred fuel for our bodies is carbohydrates. So when people tell us that they don't eat carbs, it's all we can do to maintain our cool. However, not all carbs are created equal. We need the right types of carbs—in the right amounts. There are two types of carbs: complex carbs and simple carbs.

Complex carbs are in foods such as whole grains, vegetables, and starches from potatoes. These are the "good" carbs and ones that we need for energy to fuel our body's functions.

Simple carbs are in foods such as processed grains, processed sugars, and other "junk" foods. These break down faster in the system and spike your blood sugar, and they are void of any nutrients.

Don't reject a packaged product just because it has carbs. Check the ingredients list, and make sure that the carbs are coming from healthy, complex carbs.

SUGAR

The amount of sugar mentioned on the nutrition label does not tell you the source of those sugars. To learn more, check the ingredients list. Maybe the sugars are coming from raisins or other fruits, which is okay. But maybe the sugars are coming from processed white sugar, which is not okay.

A general rule for sugars is that if a sugar is mentioned within the first three ingredients, put the product back on the shelf. But you have to look for more than just the word "sugar."

Food manufacturers are clever about using different names for refined sugars. Here are some other names you should look for that are sources of sugar that should be avoided or that should be present in very small amounts.

* **Corn syrup or corn starch**

* **Evaporated cane juice**

* **Malted barley**

* **Maple syrup**

* **Molasses**

* **Rice syrup**

* **Words ending in "ol"—such as maltitol, xylitol, and sorbitol**

* **Words ending in "ose"—such as dextrose, fructose, sucrose, and glucose**

Sugars should not be more than 5 percent of the total calories, or 2 tablespoons (13 g) per day for adults. Sugars from fruits or fruit juices are fine. Of course, everyone deserves a treat now and then, so go ahead and enjoy a cookie or two, just don't make it a daily habit, and make sure that treat is made with bone-char free sugar. (See "The Secret Animal Ingredients Hiding in Your Food" on page 60).

PROTEIN

The last nutrient to watch for is protein. If you're trying to follow a plant-based diet, you want to make sure that the protein is not coming from an animal source. We suggest that you only need between 5 and 10 percent of your daily calories from protein.

THE SECRET ANIMAL INGREDIENTS HIDING IN YOUR FOOD

From albumin to zinc hydrolyzed animal proteins, animal ingredients sneak into the foods we eat. That's why it's important to read labels and understand exactly what it is we are putting into our bodies.

Here's a list of common animal ingredients in food. It's certainly not an all-inclusive list, so keep a lookout for more. Some of the ingredients listed below also have plant-based substitutes, and we've noted them here.

* **Albumin or albumen:** Generally derived from egg whites. Used as a coagulating agent.

* **Anchovies:** Fish, often found in dressings, barbecue sauces, and Worcestershire sauce.

* **Bone char:** Charcoal made from animal bones. Used in the cane sugar refining process.

* **Capric acid:** Liquid fatty acid from cow or goat milk; can also be derived from palm or coconut oil. Used in soaps and perfumes.

* **Carmine:** A red food coloring (natural red #4) that's made from crushed insects.

* **Casein:** A protein found in milk.

* **Chitosan:** Fiber from the shells of crustaceans. Used as a fat binder in hair and skin products, as well as in "diet" foods as a fat replacer.

* **Clarifying agent or fining agent:** Can be gelatin or isinglass, generally made with fish scales, bones, or cartilage. Used to prevent cloudiness in beverages such as beer and wine.

* **Cochineal:** Another red colorant made from crushed insects.

* **Gelatin:** Made from cartilage of animal bones. Used as a thickener.

* **Glycerides, mono-, di-, and tri-:** Used in soaps and as an emulsifier.

* **Glycerols or glycerine:** Produced from oils and fats, glycerols and glycerines can be made from animal or vegetable sources. In foods and beverages, glycerol serves as a humectant, solvent, and sweetener, and may help preserve foods.

* **Isinglass:** Except Japanese isinglass, which is made from agar, made from fish scales and/or bones. Used as a clarifying agent in beverages such as beer and wine.

* **Keratin:** Protein from the ground-up horns, hooves, feathers, quills, and hair of various animals. Used in hair rinses, shampoos, and permanent wave solutions.

* **Lactic acid:** Found in blood and muscle tissue; used in sour milk, beer, sauerkraut, pickles, and other food products made by bacterial fermentation. Synthetic plant-based sources can be found.

* **Lactose:** The sugar found in milk.

* **Lanolin:** A product of the oil glands of sheep, extracted from their wool. Used as an emollient in many skin-care products and cosmetics and in medicines. Also found in chewing gum and products with vitamin D_3.

* **Lard:** Pig fat; used in many food and cooking applications.

* **Lipase:** Enzyme from the stomachs and tongue glands of calves, kids, and lambs. Used in digestive aids because it helps the body break down fats. Also commonly found in cheese and dairy products.

* **Magnesium stearate:** Manufactured from both animal and vegetable oils. Used to bind sugar in hard candies such as mints, and is a common ingredient in baby formulas.

* **Myristic acid or tetradecanoic acid:** In most animal and vegetable fats and in butter acids. Used in shampoos, creams, cosmetics, and food flavorings.

* **Natural flavorings:** Because there are no laws requiring natural flavorings to be disclosed, it's important to know that whenever this is listed as an ingredient, it can be just about anything that occurs in nature.

* **Oleic or oleinic acid:** From various animal and vegetable fats and oils, is usually obtained commercially from inedible tallow, sometimes synthesized from petroleum. Used in foods, soft soaps, bar soaps, permanent wave solutions, shampoos, creams, nail polish, lipsticks, liquid makeups, and many other skin preparations.

* **Palmitic acid:** Fatty acids from animal and plant sources. Used in shaving creams, soaps, and shampoos.

* **Pancreatin:** A mixture of several digestive enzymes produced by the exocrine cells of the pancreas. Used in nutritional supplements and in some contact lens solutions.

* **Pepsin:** Like rennett (see below), but made from pig stomachs. Used in cheese-making.

* **Propolis:** Tree sap gathered by bees and used as a sealant in beehives. Used in toothpaste, shampoo, deodorant, and nutritional supplements.

* **Rennet:** Made from thin slices of dried calf stomachs. Used in cheese-making.

* **Royal jelly:** Secretion from the throat glands of the honeybee workers that is fed to the larvae in a colony and to all queen larvae. Sold as a nutritional supplement.

* **Shellac (resinous glaze, confectioner's glaze):** Resinous excretion of certain insects. Used as a candy glaze, in hair lacquer, and on jewelry.

* **Shortening:** Unless specifically noted as vegetable shortening, can be made from lard or butter.

* **Silk:** The shiny fiber made by silkworms to form their cocoons. Worms are boiled in their cocoons to get the silk.

* **Sodium stearoyl lactylate:** Found in blood and muscle tissue. Used in sour milk, beer, sauerkraut, pickles, and other food products made by bacterial fermentation. Synthetic plant-based sources can be found.

* **Stearic acid or octadecanoic acid:** Rendered animal fat. Used as a stabilizer; found in many cosmetics.

* **Suet:** Raw beef or mutton fat, especially the hard fat found around the loins and kidneys. Used mainly in the production of tallow (see below), but is also an ingredient in cooking.

* **Tallow:** Rendered beef fat, found in many waxed papers, but not Reynold's brand.

* **Vitamin A:** Retinol acetate, is an animal-derived form of vitamin A, often added to foods, supplements, and body care products. Palmitate can be derived from animals or plants, so be sure to check the source.

* **Vitamin D:** Calciferol and cholecalciferol are names for vitamin D found in many supplements such as fish liver oil, cod liver oil, and can also be derived from beef liver and eggs. Vegan sources are available from lichens.

* **Whey:** A protein found in milk.

* **Zinc hydrolyzed animal protein:** Used in cosmetics, especially shampoos and hair treatments.

unsweetened almond milk

Simple Supermarket Swaps

One of the biggest fears folks face when deciding to make the switch to a plant-based diet is the fear of never enjoying certain favorite foods again. The truth is, it's never been easier to be a vegetarian or vegan. The popularity of plant-based eating has food producers taking notice. As one of the largest growing sectors of the food service industry, more and more vegan products are becoming available at traditional grocery stores. Here are some super-easy supermarket swaps that will make a meatless meal a no-brainer.

MILK AND DAIRY PRODUCTS

This one is the easiest of all. In most grocery stores, right next to the traditional cow's milk, you'll find a variety of nondairy milks. The most common is soymilk. In addition, you'll find coconut milk, almond milk, rice milk, and even hemp milk. All of these varieties typically come in several flavors, such as original, unsweetened, vanilla, and sometimes even chocolate.

You're not limited to just milks. Many of the same companies that make nondairy milks also make nondairy yogurts, sour cream, creamers for coffee, and ice cream–like desserts. Products such as whipped dessert topping in a can are available in rice and soy varieties as well. And if butter is your poison, you'll find nondairy buttery spreads that taste so good, they'll make you wonder why you ever liked dairy in the first place.

The main thing to look for in choosing nondairy milks and other products is taste! Try out different brands and different flavors until you find one that you love. And remember, different milks work well for different uses. For instance, you may love vanilla rice milk by the glass, but you might find that unsweetened almond milk produces much better results when baking.

CHEESE

Ahh, cheese. This is the dairy product that most people have the hardest time giving up. After all, it's melty and gooey, and it tastes so good on nachos. We have experienced that suggesting people give up cheese is a little like asking them to remove a body part! But we are here to tell you that there is life after cheese—really, a much healthier one.

Years ago when we started our healthy journey, the cheese substitutes were really not very good. Plus, the most entertaining thing to Gerrie was that the cheese substitutes would use caseinate in the products to give them the meltability and consistency of real cheese. Caseinate is the protein found in dairy—so why in the world would manufacturers put a dairy protein in a cheese substitute?

It takes 1.5 gallons (5.5 l) of milk to make 1 pound (454 g) of cheese. So giving up dairy milk means you also need to give up cheese, or at least replace it with other options in recipes.

It used to be that you either made your own nut-based cheese at home, or you simply did without, because store-bought vegan cheeses were, honestly, just gross. But, guess what? The vegan food industry, along with some amazing and talented vegan chefs, have made great strides in producing melty, stringy, and downright tasty dairy-free cheeses in the past few years. Every new product that comes out is better than the last.

Look for brands such as Follow Your Heart's Vegan Gourmet, Daiya, Kite Hill, Teese, Tofutti, Nacheez, Queso for Lovers, Parmela, Parma, Nutty Cow, and many more. Several brands of shredded vegan cheeses are available and perfect on a pizza, in a burrito, for grilled cheese sandwiches, and, of course, as a topping for nachos. If you are limiting (or eliminating) added oil from your diet, these options should be used very sparingly or not at all.

You can buy cream cheese alternatives in plain and flavors like strawberry, cinnamon, and even garlic herb, which are perfect for spreading on crackers and bagels. Solid cheeses that mimic cheddar, Swiss, and other traditional favorites are also available. Add in any number of the aged nut-based cheeses now available, and you can make yourself a delicious cheese plate to share and enjoy at your next cocktail party. From aged Parmesan sprinkles to brie, artisan vegan cheese has made a name for itself even in the traditional cheese-making realm.

These new plant-based cheeses melt and taste pretty close to traditional dairy cheeses and work really well as cheese substitutes in your favorite recipes. Also, check out our recipe section starting on page 71 for some wonderful recipes that include plant-based cheese.

EGGS

Substituting eggs can be a little bit trickier than all the rest. What you're planning to do with the egg will determine how best to swap it out. For example, if you want to make a scrambled egg dish, omelet, deviled eggs, or egg salad, tofu is your swap of choice.

However, if you're baking a batch of cookies, cupcakes, or a custard, you may want to use a commercial egg replacer such as Ener-G or Bob's Red Mill, which both use a blend of flours you mix with water to make a whipped-like concoction to replace beaten eggs in recipes.

Does egg replacer powder sound a little too "out there" for you? That's okay, you can survive without it. Many recipes turn out just fine using a little ground flaxseed mixed with warm water, applesauce (or other fruit purée), or some blended silken tofu to replace an egg.

CHICKEN AND BEEF

Looking to replace chicken breast in a recipe? No problem, just pick up a package of Beyond Meat in the refrigerated section or Gardein in the frozen aisle.

Looking for a tasty alternative to beef? Upton's or WestSoy Seitan, Gimme Lean Gardein Beefless Tips, or their Ultimate Beefless Patties are spot-on replacements for the real thing. Maybe you're after a nice spicy chorizo sausage? El Burrito has you covered with its delicious version of Soyrizo.

Looking to grill up some hot dogs or brats at your next cookout? Field Roast, Tofurkey, Yves, and Smart Pups all make prepackaged ready-to-cook hot dogs and sausages ready for the grill.

Or maybe you just need a package of sliced deli meat to make school lunches. Head on over to the refrigerated section of your local health food store. Right next to the tofu, you'll find packaged Yves or Tofurky brand deli slices flavored and spiced to mimic salami, turkey, and even bologna!

It's pretty amazing what companies have been able to do with plant proteins. Use these products just as you would their animal-based counterparts in recipes. You'll be hard pressed to notice a difference.

HONEY

This one is super easy. Agave syrup can be used to replace honey at a one-for-one ratio in recipes. If you have an aversion to agave, you can use any number of other liquid sweeteners to replace honey, such as brown rice syrup, maple syrup, or molasses. Of course, these syrups have their own distinct flavors, so we recommend experimenting to find your favorite. As an alternative, you can use a variety of fruits or fruit juices as unrefined sweeteners.

CONVENIENCE FOODS

Maybe you're a busy bee, and a frozen dinner is about all you have time for with your hectic schedule. Fret not! Tofurky, Daiya, Gardein, and Amy's brands tout vegan versions of everything, including frozen burritos, macaroni and cheese, frozen pizzas, hot pockets, and full-blown replicas of your favorite TV dinner. But be careful of those sodium, sugar, and oils when purchasing ready-made convenience foods.

Pantry Basics: A Guide to "Weird" Vegan Ingredients

In this book and any other vegan cookbook out there, you'll find ingredients that may be new to you. The following quick rundown will help you understand what some of these ingredients are!

AGAR FLAKES AND POWDER

Also known as *kanten,* this all-vegetable gelatin is derived from red algae. It's commonly used throughout Asia to thicken soups, desserts, and jellies. Most often, it is found in flake or powder form. If you search for it, you can also find it in sticks or rods that can be ground down to your desired consistency. To assure the right amount gets used, we will always give the weight when calling for this ingredient in recipes.

BEANS

As a convenience, we like to use canned beans, choosing the "no salt added" varieties when available or rinsing and draining them thoroughly to get rid of unnecessary sodium. If you cook your own dried beans, more power to you! Keep in mind that one 15-ounce (425 g) can of beans generally equals approximately 1⅔ cups (294 g) cooked beans, or ⅔ cup (120 g) dry beans.

COCONUT MILK AND COCONUT CREAM

Generally, when we call for coconut milk in a recipe, we recommend the full-fat variety. It's usually found in a can in the international aisle of most grocery stores. If left unshaken, the coconut cream will separate from the coconut water. This thick, delicious cream is also called for in some recipes. Luckily, you can also buy just the cream! If you are watching your fat intake, go easy on coconut milk because it is high in saturated fat.

FLOURS

For the sake of accuracy in measurements, we use a scoop to transfer flour into the measuring cup, so as not to overpack it. It can make a difference in how recipes turn out, so it's a good thing to keep in mind. We choose the flour based on the flavor profile of the recipe, and whenever possible, we choose 100 percent whole grain flours.

JACKFRUIT

When this starchy fruit is ripe, it has a very mild flavor that's similar to a cross between a pineapple and a banana. When the fruit is young and green, it takes on the flavors of whatever you cook with it. As it cooks, it breaks down into a stringy, almost meaty texture, which makes it a perfect medium for dishes simulating "pulled pork" or "shredded chicken."

It's almost impossible to find fresh jackfruit. When you do, it's almost always well ripened and too sweet for most applications in this book, so we stick to the canned variety, packed in brine (not syrup) for savory recipes.

LIQUID SMOKE

In most markets, this flavoring is stocked near the marinades. It's actually made by condensing smoke into liquid form. A little goes a long way in giving a smoky flavor to many foods.

MISO

This pungent paste has a variety of uses. It makes a very versatile and simple broth, and a little bit added to sauces, stews, and even cheese sauces adds depth of flavor and sharpness. You can find it in most Asian grocery stores and sometimes in your local health food store in the refrigerated section.

NONDAIRY MILKS

We most commonly use unsweetened soymilk, almond milk, or coconut milk when cooking. They seem to give the best results. However, if you have a preference for another type of nondairy milk, we are sure it will work just fine. We recommend using one of these three in any recipes where a "buttermilk" texture is needed.

NUTRITIONAL YEAST

Ahh, the nooch. This flaky yellow yeast is usually grown on molasses. It has a nutty, rich, almost cheesy flavor that also adds a nutritional boost to your foods. (Hello, B vitamins!) Be sure to seek out "vegetarian support" formulas. You can find nutritional yeast in the vitamin and supplement section of most health food stores. This yeast is of the non-active variety and can be enjoyed by people with candida. Don't confuse it with brewer's yeast. They will yield very different results in recipes.

SALT AND PEPPER

We respect your habits when it comes to salt and pepper, so the measurements you'll find in many of our recipes are meant as a guide. We usually add "to taste" so that you can follow your needs and preferences. We prefer using sea salt because it retains a minuscule amount of minerals. We like to use a small amount of black salt in recipes that replicate eggs, because it lends a delicate, sulfurous flavor to foods.

SEAWEED

Edible seaweeds, such as hijiki, dulse, and nori, add a fishy and salty flavor to foods without using fish. Most can be found in your local health food store or Asian supermarket.

SOY SAUCE, TAMARI, BRAGG LIQUID AMINOS, AND COCONUT AMINOS

These ingredients can be used interchangeably in recipes. It really is personal taste preference. For people with gluten sensitivities, wheat-free tamari and Bragg's are usually good choices. Bragg's is also lower in sodium than traditional soy sauce.

SRIRACHA OR "ROOSTER SAUCE"

Made from chile peppers, garlic, vinegar, and salt ground together to form a smooth paste, this hot sauce is addictive. Check for ingredients, because some brands contain fish sauce.

SUGAR

We don't use refined white sugar in any of our recipes. Most refined white sugar is processed using charred animal bones. We prefer to keep the bones out of our sugar, so we stick with the more natural, cruelty-free versions. When shopping, look for evaporated cane juice, raw sugar, or turbinado sugar. These sugars are slightly off white in color. They still contain some trace minerals that are otherwise completely removed through the sugar refining process. If you really need pure white sugar, use beet sugar, which does not go through the same refining process as cane sugar, or white sugar that is clearly labeled as vegan. To reduce the amount of added sugar, you can also use dates or dried fruit pastes. This way you also get the nutritional benefits of the fruit, such as fiber, vitamins, and minerals.

TEMPEH

Whole soybeans fermented and pressed into a cake, tempeh is considered to be healthier and less processed than tofu, with an earthier flavor. Although tempeh is available in a wide variety of shapes and sizes, we try to stick with the plain variety.

For people who find the flavor a bit too much to handle, extra or super firm tofu can usually be used as a substitute in recipes. Bitter to some, this whole-bean soy treat is a very versatile protein. Still afraid? Simmer tempeh in water or vegetable broth for about 20 minutes prior to using in recipes. It mellows the flavor.

TOFU

We call for soft silken tofu in a lot of recipes because it makes a great base for desserts and creamy sauces. In this case, you can use the kind packaged in aseptic shelf-stable packaging or fresh packed in water. We also call for extra- or super-firm tofu in a lot of recipes where the tofu will be the main star of the dish. In this case, refrigerated types are recommended.

If you're lucky enough to live near an Asian grocery that sells fresh tofu, buy it! It's so much better than pre-packaged tofu.

When using extra- or super-firm tofu, it is always best to drain and press it ahead of time, to save time when preparing the recipes. One of the easiest ways to do this is to sandwich the block of tofu between folded kitchen towels or a few layers of paper towels and then place a heavy pan or book on top to press out excess moisture.

VEGETABLE BROTH

Everyone has their own favorite brand, and Joni's is Better Than Bouillon. It comes in several flavors: Better than Chicken, Better than Beef, and Vegetable. It's a small jar of bouillon paste that has fantastic flavor, and she cannot recommend it highly enough. She also loves to keep a stockpile of veggie broth powder on hand to use in spice mixes and other recipes.

Because Gerrie does not use extracted oils in her food, she's a big fan of the Pacifica, low-sodium vegetable broth. This is one of the few veggies broths that doesn't have oil in it. Even bouillon cubes have oil added, so if you are cutting out extracted oils, read the labels!

Of course, you can make your own low-sodium broth. Simply save all of those veggie scraps you'd normally throw out, add them to a pot, cover with water, bring to a boil, reduce to a simmer, and cook for two hours. Strain out the solids and use as desired.

VEGETABLE OIL

As a general rule, we'll always try to give alternatives to using oils when warranted. That being said, Joni believes there is still a valuable use of oil in a vegan diet. When recipes call for a mild-flavored vegetable oil, Joni generally uses canola, but she knows many of you don't. She also uses coconut oil quite often, but she understands it can be cost prohibitive. Extra-virgin olive oil is often used when the flavor of the oil needs to shine through, as in salad dressings. Peanut is also a favorite when she is frying, because it has a very high smoke point. Unless specifically noted in a recipe, use whichever mild-flavored vegetable oil you prefer.

Gerrie doesn't use any oils in her cooking, and she has found the flavors to be just as delicious. In fact, oils can mask the taste and flavors of foods, so most dishes prepared without oil are more flavorful and definitely contain far fewer calories. Also, because oils are not cheap, minimizing them is another way you can cut down your grocery costs.

VITAL WHEAT GLUTEN FLOUR

Gluten is the natural protein portion removed from whole wheat. You can find vital wheat gluten flour in most grocery stores or order it online. It's important to know that vital wheat gluten flour is completely different from high-gluten flour. The two are not interchangeable, and they won't perform the same in recipes.

Shelf-Stable Staples No Vegan Should Be Without

The following is a list of ingredients regularly used in plant-based recipes that will last for a long time in your pantry.

Flours

* All-purpose flour
* Chickpea flour
* Vital wheat gluten flour
* Whole wheat flour
* Whole wheat pastry flour

Dried beans

* Black beans
* Chickpeas
* Red beans

Dried grains

* Buckwheat
* Farro
* Oats
* Quinoa
* Rice

Dried spices

* Allspice
* Anise
* Basil
* Cinnamon
* Cumin
* Curry
* Fennel
* Garlic
* Parsley
* Rosemary
* Sage
* Thyme
* Turmeric

Organic textured vegetable protein

POWDERED EGG REPLACERS

* Bob's Red Mill
* Ener-G
* Vegg

SEAWEEDS

* Arame
* Dulse
* Hijiki
* Kelp
* Kombu
* Nori
* Wakame

Soy or hemp protein powders

STARCH POWDERS

* Arrowroot
* Cornstarch
* Potato Starch

VEGETABLE BROTH POWDER OR BOUILLON

Let's Get Started

We've now armed you with all of the knowledge and information necessary to shop for just about anything you'll need to create healthy and cruelty-free dishes in your very own vegan kitchen. Are you ready to get cooking? We hope so! The next two chapters are full of recipes and meal plans designed to make your conversion to WellBeing an easy and tasty one.

Chapter 6

The Recipes

We've given you the *why* for going vegan, and now it's time
for us to give you the *how* so you can cook up some delicious and nutritious vegan food that's guaranteed to get you closer to WellBeing!

All of these recipes are designed to get your feet wet in a vegan
kitchen. They're jumping-off points—meant to be used as guidelines. Try
them out, and then make adjustments to them so they're truly your own.

GUIDE TO RECIPE DESCRIPTIONS

We've done our best to label the recipes in this book with the following labels:

* **Soy free:** These recipes do not include ingredients containing soy.

* **Gluten free:** These recipes do not include ingredients containing gluten.

* **Nut free:** These recipes contain no nuts.

* **No added oil:** These recipes have no added refined oils.

* **No added salt:** These recipes have no added salt.

* **No added sugar:** These recipes have no added refined sugar or sweeteners.

* **Quick and easy:** These recipes take fewer than 30 minutes to prepare.

A note about allergies: However careful we may be, allergens have a way of sneaking into products that we might otherwise think are safe. Different brands may include some ingredients that are not present in the brands that we use, so please be diligent in checking ingredient labels when cooking for yourself or others who may suffer from certain food allergies. After all, this is a book about feeling great with the food we eat, and the last thing we would want is for someone to get sick.

You'll also see "Veggie Bite" sidebars throughout this chapter. These are tidbits of information that we thought would be helpful or fun.

Crispy Toaster Waffles

* Soy free
* Nut free
* No added oil
* No added salt

Yield: 6 to 8 waffles

We love crispy waffles, and the addition of rice flour makes these waffles nice and crispy. We cook up the whole batch and then freeze the leftovers so we can just pop them into the toaster for a quick breakfast during the week.

¼ cup (26 g) ground flax seeds

¾ cup (180 ml) warm water

1½ cups (180 g) whole wheat flour

½ cup (79 g) rice flour

½ cup (100 g) date paste or maple syrup

2 teaspoons vanilla extract

1 teaspoon ground cinnamon

1 cup (235 ml) water or unsweetened almond milk

In a bowl, mix flaxseeds and warm water. Set aside to thicken. (For a quicker preparation, place flaxseeds and water into a hot pan and cook for approximately 4 minutes over medium heat, stirring constantly, until mixture because gelatinous, similar to an egg white.)

In another bowl, mix whole wheat flour and rice flour. Once the flaxseed mixture has thickened, pour into bowl with flours, date paste or maple syrup, vanilla extract, and cinnamon. Stir in water or almond milk until mixture has a batter consistency. (It should be thick, but still pourable.)

Now pour the mixture into your waffle maker, cook, and enjoy!

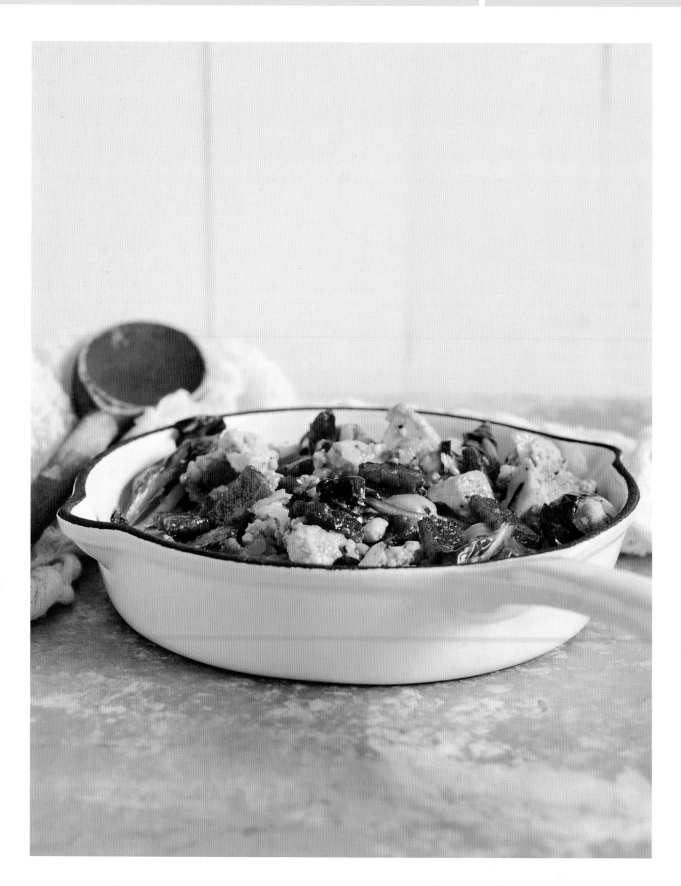

Down-Home Country Tofu Scramble

No self-respecting book titled *Going Vegan* would be complete without a recipe for a tofu scramble! And this one doesn't disappoint. One thing Joni really missed when she went vegan was a big, hearty skillet breakfast, so she came up with this recipe, using potatoes, tofu, and tempeh to recreate a healthier vegan version of one of her favorites from a well-known twenty-four-hour diner.

1 block (10 to 12 ounces, or 280 to 340 g) extra- or super-firm tofu, pressed and drained

¼ cup (30 g) nutritional yeast

½ teaspoon turmeric

1 tablespoon (11 g) Dijon mustard

2 tablespoons (28 ml) oil, optional, or vegetable broth

2 cups (220 g) shredded potatoes, rinsed in cool water to remove excess starch

1 medium yellow onion, julienne cut

1 tablespoon (10 g) minced garlic

½ recipe, "Sweet and Smoky Tempeh Strips" (see page 87), cut into bite-size chunks

1 cup (30 g) baby spinach or any other green

Pinch black salt, optional, plus more to taste

Salt, to taste

Ground black pepper, to taste

In a small bowl, crumble tofu and toss with nutritional yeast, turmeric, and mustard to coat.

In large skillet, heat oil or broth, if using, over medium-high heat. Add potatoes and onion. Sauté about 5 minutes, tossing constantly.

Add garlic and continue to cook an additional 2 to 3 minutes, or until garlic is fragrant and onion is translucent.

Add tofu and chopped tempeh strips and toss to mix. Continue to cook an additional 5 minutes, or until tofu is heated through.

Remove from heat and toss in spinach to wilt. Add black salt and toss. Add salt and pepper, to taste

VEGGIE BITE

Tofu Scramble can also be made into an awesome breakfast or brunch casserole by tossing together all the ingredients and spreading in a 9 × 9-inch (23 × 23 cm) baking dish. Sprinkle the top with your favorite shredded nondairy cheese and bake at 350°F (180°C, or gas mark 4), covered with foil, for 30 minutes. Remove foil and bake an additional 20 minutes, until top is slightly browned and most of the liquid has evaporated.

Loaded Oatmeal

* Quick and easy   Yield: 4 hearty servings

2 cups (156 g) quick cooking oats

2 tablespoons (13 g) ground flax seeds

2 tablespoons (12 g) ground hemp seeds or hearts, optional

½ teaspoon ground cinnamon

1 apple, peeled (optional), cored, and diced

1 banana, peeled and sliced

2 cups (470 ml) almond or coconut milk

2 cups (470 ml) water

1 cup (220 g) brown sugar, tightly packed, divided, optional

1 teaspoon vanilla extract

1 cup (145 g) fresh or frozen blueberries

½ cup (120 ml) maple syrup

½ cup (55 g) sliced or slivered almonds

If you're looking for a quick-and-easy way to make a big impact on your family's breakfast, you've found it! Made with only one pot and virtually mess free, this energy-packed breakfast can be on the table in 10 minutes flat.

In a large pot with tight-fitting lid, add oats, flax, hemp, if using, cinnamon, apple, banana, milk, water, and ½ cup brown sugar. Stir to combine. Cover and heat over medium heat, until oatmeal begins to bubble. Stir in vanilla and continue to cook about 5 minutes, until soft and hot.

Remove from heat. Stir in blueberries. Spoon into serving bowls and top with remaining brown sugar, maple syrup, and almonds.

VEGGIE BITE

Looking for even more oomph in your oatmeal? Mix in one scoop of vanilla-flavored protein powder at the same time you stir in the blueberries. There are soy, hemp, and even rice based protein powders available.

Creamy Quinoa Breakfast Cereal

* Soy free
* No added oil
* No added salt
* No added sugar   Yield: 6 large servings

Quinoa is a great breakfast alternative when you want something different. Quinoa is higher in protein than oats, and it has a very pleasant taste. You can still add all the yummy things that work in oatmeal, as well. Feel free to improvise with this recipe to your taste.

1 pound (454 g) quinoa

6 cups (1.4 L) vanilla-flavored, unsweetened almond milk

1 tablespoon (8 g) ground cinnamon

1 cup (145 g) raisins

Quinoa must be thoroughly rinsed before cooking. Use a fine mesh strainer and pour in quinoa. Rinse with cold water until the water runs clear.

In a large pot, combine rinsed quinoa, almond milk, cinnamon, and raisins. Place on low heat (do not let it boil) until quinoa is cooked (grain will open when done) and raisins have become very soft. Remove from heat and serve.

VEGGIE BITE

You can add fresh berries, apples, or your other favorite fruits to top the cereal in your bowl. Alternate fruits for different flavor variations.

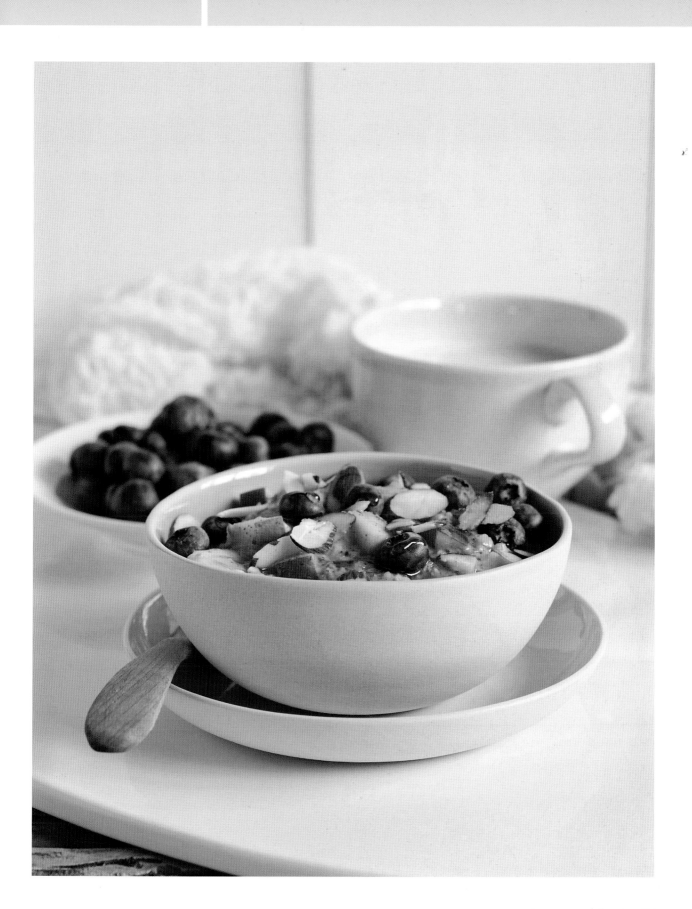

Spinach and Mushroom Eggless Benedict

* Soy free
* Nut free
* No added oil
* No added salt
* No added sugar

Yield: 6 servings

This is a little different (better!) than the traditional Benedicts. It's a delicious dish that can be served for breakfast—or any time of the day.

1 large yellow onion, diced

3 fresh garlic cloves, minced

1 large leek, cleaned and sliced

¼ cup (60 ml) no-oil, low-sodium vegetable broth

1 cup (70 g) sliced white or button mushrooms

2 cups (60 g) fresh or frozen spinach, chopped if you like smaller pieces

1 teaspoon no-salt vegetable seasoning

½ teaspoon ground black pepper

1 teaspoon ground nutmeg

1 teaspoon dried thyme

1 teaspoon dried oregano

3 whole-grain English muffins

2 fresh tomatoes, sliced in ½-inch rounds

1 ripe avocado, cut into long, thin slices

1 cup (235 ml) Al-Mond-Fredo Sauce (see page 137)

Nutritional yeast, to taste

In a hot pan, add onion, garlic, and leek and cook until onion and leek become translucent, soft, and begin to caramelize.

Add vegetable broth to lift caramelization off bottom of pan and to add extra flavor. Cook 2 minutes.

Then add mushrooms and cook until soft and moisture comes out of mushrooms. Stir in spinach, vegetable seasoning, pepper, nutmeg, thyme, and oregano, and continue to cook until moisture evaporates.

Cut English muffins in half and toast in toaster. For each serving, place muffin half on plate. Put fresh slice of tomato on muffin. Top tomato with cooked spinach mixture. Then place two or three slices of avocado on top of spinach and drizzle with Al-Mond-Fredo Sauce. Sprinkle with nutritional yeast and *enjoy*!

....

VEGGIE BITE

Vegetable seasoning is made from dried vegetables with no salt added.

....

Gerrie's Favorite Breakfast Skillet

* Soy free
* Gluten free
* Nut free
* No added oil
* No added salt
* No added sugar

Yield: 4 servings

This is Gerrie's favorite breakfast. It fulfills her need for a big, hearty breakfast. It is also what she will order when she eats out with her family on weekends. Here is how you make it at home. Enjoy!

3 or 4 Yukon gold or red potatoes with skins on

1 white onion, diced

1 yellow onion, diced

1 tablespoon (10 g) minced garlic

Low-sodium, no-oil vegetable broth, as needed

1 red bell pepper, seeded and diced

1 green bell pepper, seeded and diced

1 yellow bell pepper, seeded and diced

5 ounces (140 g) baby spinach

1 package (8 ounces, or 227 g) sliced mushrooms

1 teaspoon turmeric

1 teaspoon ground black pepper

1 tablespoon nutritional yeast

Low-sodium salsa

Clean potato skins and chop into bite-size pieces. Steam or bake until potato starts to soften. Set aside.

While potato is cooking, heat large skillet. Place onion and garlic in skillet. Stir while cooking to prevent sticking. If caramelization begins, splash in small amount of low-sodium veggie broth.

When onions turn translucent, add bell peppers. Cook approximately 5 minutes, or until peppers soften. Add spinach and mushrooms. Cook for another 5 minutes, or until spinach wilts and mushrooms become soft.

Fold in cooked potatoes and season with turmeric, black pepper, and nutritional yeast. (Adjust amount to fit your tastes as necessary.) Allow mixture to cook until it is heated throughout. Top with salsa and serve.

VEGGIE BITE

If ordering from a restaurant, simply order the vegetable omelet and tell them to hold the egg and cheese. Ask that the potatoes be placed on a dry grill with all of the vegetables and heated until all ingredients are soft. Order a side of salsa, and you are good to go!

Drink Your Greens Smoothie

Yield: 2 servings

This recipe is inspired by one of Gerrie's teachers, Dr. Joel Fuhrman. It's a great recipe to get a lot of greens even if you are green-phobic.

1 banana

5 ounces (140 g) baby spinach

8 ounces (227 g) frozen blueberries

2 cups (470 ml) unsweetened Almond milk

1 cup (255 g) frozen strawberries

1 tbsp (7 g) flaxseeds

Add all ingredients to a blender and puree until smooth.

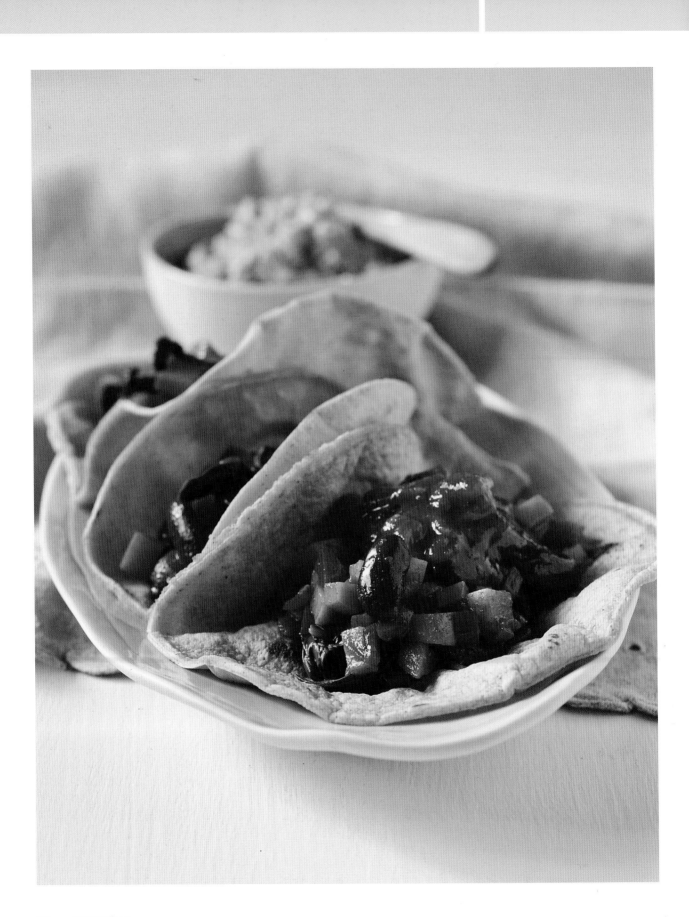

Veggie-Good Breakfast Tacos

* Soy free
* Gluten free
* Nut free
* No added oil
* No added salt
* No added sugar

Yield: 12 tacos

This is a delicious way to start a weekend day! Potatoes and vegetables provide a delicious way to fill you up with lots of nutrients and keep you going for hours. Plus when you add avocado, corn tortillas, and salsa, it makes for a breakfast delight. (Note that this recipe will be gluten free as long as you use gluten-free tortillas and broth.)

5 cloves garlic, chopped

1 cup (160 g) diced onion

Low-sodium, oil-free vegetable broth, enough to keep onions from sticking

1 red bell pepper, seeded and chopped

2½ pounds (1107 g) Yukon gold potatoes, cut into ¼-inch (6 mm) cubes and boiled until fork tender

½ teaspoon ground black pepper

1 tablespoon (3 g) ancho or chipotle chili powder

1 can (15 ounces, or 378 g) no-sodium-added black or kidney beans, rinsed and drained

1 cup (225 g) baby spinach

12 (6-inch, or 15 cm) organic corn tortillas

2 ripe avocados, chopped

1 cup (235 ml) salsa

Heat a large saucepan, then place garlic and onion in pan. Cook approximately 5 minutes, or until onions become translucent. Splash a little veggie broth in the pan if onions start to stick.

Once onion becomes soft, add red pepper, potatoes, black pepper, and chili powder. Continue cooking until pepper softens, approximately 5 minutes.

Add beans and cook until heated through, 2 to 3 minutes.

Add spinach and cook until wilted, 3 to 4 minutes.

With a tortilla warmer, heat tortillas. (If you don't have a tortilla steamer/warmer, see "Veggie Bites" below.)

To assemble, add potatoes and spinach mixture to corn tortilla and then top with avocado and salsa.

....

VEGGIE BITES

If you don't have a tortilla warmer, it's something you should consider investing in. A tortilla warmer keeps your tortillas warm while you're working on your first taco and preparing your second one!

If you don't have a tortilla warmer, you can use this alternate method. Get two salad plates. Place the tortillas on one plate. Wrap them with a damp paper towel and then top with the second plate, face down. Microwave on high for 3 minutes, and the tortillas will come out nice and steamy. To keep the tortillas warm, leave the damp paper towel wrapped around the tortillas and wrap all with aluminum foil.

If you don't like to use microwaves, you can use an indoor grill to warm the tortillas. Place as many tortillas as possible on the grill for approximately 1 minute on each side. When the tortillas are warm, wrap them in a piece of aluminum foil.

....

Chilaquiles Roja

* Gluten free
* Nut free

Yield: 4 servings

Chilaquiles are kinda like breakfast nachos. This version calls for a mole for the sauce and pre-made tortilla chips. If you're following a no-oil diet, you can make your own baked, oil-free chips and simply eliminate the oil in the recipe by using a good nonstick pan when cooking the onions and garlic. Also, we used canned beans. If you prefer to cook your own beans, you'll need 1¾ cups (15 ounces, or 425 g) cooked beans, plus ¼ cup (60 ml) of the cooking liquid.

FOR MOLE:

1 tablespoon (15 ml) vegetable oil

½ cup (80 g) diced white onion

2 teaspoons minced garlic

½ to 1 teaspoon (more or less to taste) dried red chili flakes or chili powder

¼ teaspoon chipotle powder or cayenne pepper

½ teaspoon smoked paprika

1 can (15 ounces, or 425 g) tomato sauce

1 whole star anise

1 cinnamon stick

2 whole allspice

¼ cup (44 g) semi-sweet nondairy chocolate chips

1 shot (1 fluid ounce, or 30 ml) brewed espresso or ¾ teaspoon instant espresso powder

2 tablespoons (30 g) packed brown sugar (dark is best, but light works too)

Sea salt, to taste

Freshly ground black pepper, to taste

To make the sauce: In a pot with a tightly fitting lid, heat oil over medium high heat. Add onion and sauté until translucent.

Add garlic and cook an additional 2 to 3 minutes, or until fragrant. Add chili flakes or chili powder, chipotle powder or cayenne, and paprika. Cook 1 minute.

Add tomato sauce, star anise, cinnamon stick, allspice, chocolate chips, espresso or espresso powder, and brown sugar. Cook, stirring, until chocolate is melted. Cover, reduce heat to low, and simmer 30 minutes. Add salt and pepper, to taste. Remove anise, allspice, and cinnamon stick before serving.

For an extra-smooth sauce, use an immersion stick blender or carefully transfer mixture to a blender and blend until smooth. Keep warm until remainder of dish is ready.

To prepare the beans: In a frying pan or cast iron skillet, heat oil over high heat. Add onion and garlic. Sauté until brown, about 3 to 5 minutes. Stir in cumin, paprika, and oregano. Cook 1 minute.

Add beans, with their liquid, and reduce heat to medium low. Simmer, uncovered, 15 minutes, stirring occasionally.

Using a hand potato masher or fork, mash the mixture to desired chunkiness. Season to taste with salt and pepper. Remove from heat.

To make the tofu cotija crumbles: In a small bowl, mix tofu with lime juice, garlic powder, onion powder, oregano, cumin, chipotle powder, and salt and pepper, to taste.

To assemble the chilaquiles: On a plate or in a bowl, place a layer of beans. Carefully add two handfuls of chips to the mole and toss to get a thin coating on each chip. Place mole-covered chips on top of the beans. Top with tofu cotija crumbles. Garnish as desired. (See "Veggie Bite," below.)

FOR REFRIED BLACK BEANS:

1 tablespoon (15 ml) vegetable oil

1 cup (160 g) diced yellow or white onion

2 teaspoons minced garlic

¼ teaspoon ground cumin

¼ teaspoon smoked paprika

¼ teaspoon dried oregano

1 can (15 ounces, or 425 g) black beans, with liquid

Sea salt, to taste

Freshly ground black pepper, to taste

FOR TOFU COTIJA CRUMBLES:

1 cup (225 g) extra-firm tofu, crumbled until it resembles feta cheese

1 tablespoon (15 ml) lime juice

½ teaspoon garlic powder

½ teaspoon onion powder

½ teaspoon dried oregano

¼ teaspoon ground cumin

¼ teaspoon chipotle powder

Sea salt, to taste

Freshly ground black pepper, to taste

1 bag (16 ounces, or 454 g) tortilla chips

VEGGIE BITE

This recipe is just a start! People add all sorts of things to the top of their chilaquiles, such as nondairy sour cream, green onions, fresh avocado slices, cilantro, nondairy cheese, Walnut Chorizo (page 88), and salsa. The possibilities are endless!

Nutty Fruitcake Pancakes

FOR THE TOPPING:

½ cup (55 g) chopped pecans

¼ cup (30 g) chopped walnuts

¼ cup (26 g) sliced or slivered almonds

¼ cup (30 g) dried cranberries or raisins

¼ cup (22 g) crushed banana chips

¼ cup (30 g) sweetened or unsweetened shredded coconut

⅓ cup (80 ml) rum

1 cup (235 ml) pure maple syrup

FOR THE PANCAKES:

2 tablespoons (22 g) ground flax seed

¼ cup (60 ml) warm water

1¼ cups (295 ml) coconut milk from a carton, almond milk, or soy milk

¼ cup (60 ml) rum

2 tablespoons (30 ml) lime juice

1 cup (125 g) all-purpose flour

1 cup (120 g) whole wheat pastry flour

1 teaspoon baking powder

1 teaspoon baking soda

½ teaspoon salt

¼ teaspoon ground allspice

¼ cup (60 ml) mild-flavored vegetable oil

2 tablespoons (30 ml) maple syrup

¼ cup (26 g) sliced or slivered almonds

¼ cup (27 g) chopped pecans

¼ cup (30 g) chopped walnuts

¼ cup (10 g) freeze-dried blueberries

¼ cup (30 g) dried cranberries or raisins

¼ cup (30 g) sweetened or unsweetened shredded coconut

Normally we wouldn't advocate drinking rum at breakfast, but these fruitcake-inspired pancakes just wouldn't be the same without it! You can use spiced, light, dark, or even coconut rum in these pancakes. Also, we use 100 percent pure grade A or B maple syrup. Grade A is first run maple syrup, which is lighter in color and flavor. Grade B is second run, which is darker and much more intensely flavored. Pure maple syrup will be clearly marked as grade A or B on the label. The "good stuff" tastes really good, and it is so much better for you than the maple-flavored sugar stuff.

To make the topping: Place all topping ingredients in a bowl, give it a good stir, and set aside.

To make the pancakes: In a small bowl, mix together flax seed and water. Set aside.

In another, slightly larger bowl, mix together milk, rum, and lime juice. (The mixture will curdle and become like buttermilk.) Set aside.

In a large mixing bowl, mix together all-purpose flour, whole wheat pastry flour, baking powder, baking soda, salt, and allspice.

Stir flax mixture, oil, and syrup into milk mixture. Add this wet mixture into the flour mixture and stir to combine. Fold in almonds, pecans, walnuts, blueberries, cranberries or raisins, and coconut.

Preheat a nonstick griddle or skillet over medium heat.

Using a ⅓-cup measure, pour ⅓ cup (3.25 ounces, or 92 g) batter onto the griddle and cook as you would any pancake, or until bubbles begin to pop and edges begin to lift, then flip. Repeat with remaining batter.

Spoon topping over the top of pancake stack before serving.

....

VEGGIE BITE

Having your griddle or pan at the right temperature is crucial to a perfectly golden flapjack. On an electric stove, we found that setting #4, out of 10, on the stove's larger burner, was plenty hot. When cooking with gas, we would say a medium flame will get the job done just fine. We know cooking pancakes can be frustrating for some, so start with a tiny one to test the heat of your griddle. Usually, the pancakes after the third one on are all winners!

....

Sweet and Smoky Tempeh Strips

* Nut free   Yield: 18 to 20 pieces

No self-respecting how-to-go-vegan cookbook would be complete without a recipe for tempeh bacon. There are hundreds of them out there, some better than others. This one is perfect for making big batches and keeping on hand in the fridge. Use it whenever you crave a sweet-and-smoky strip.

1 block (8 ounces, or 227 g) plain soy tempeh

¼ cup (60 ml) maple syrup

2 tablespoons (30 ml) liquid smoke

2 tablespoons (30 ml) mild-flavored vegetable oil, optional

2 tablespoons (30 ml) soy sauce or tamari

1 tablespoon (14 g) tightly packed brown sugar

2 teaspoons apple cider vinegar

½ teaspoon salt (or to taste)

½ teaspoon ground black pepper

½ teaspoon garlic powder

½ teaspoon onion powder

¼ teaspoon smoked paprika

Steam or simmer the tempeh for 20 minutes to reduce bitterness, if desired.

Meanwhile, in a bowl, mix remaining ingredients, including the oil, if using, together to make the marinade.

Slice tempeh into thin strips. Mix tempeh and marinade in a shallow dish or a resealable plastic bag and allow to marinate for at least 1 hour in the refrigerator.

Preheat oven to 350°F (180°C, or gas mark 4). Line a rimmed baking sheet with parchment paper or reusable silicon baking mat. Arrange tempeh strips in a single layer on the sheet. Pour any excess marinade over the strips.

Bake for 15 minutes, flip, and bake for an additional 15 minutes, or until the tempeh strips are a rich chocolate-brown color, dry but still flexible.

Use immediately, or store in an airtight container in the refrigerator until ready to use. You can eat the strips cold, or reheat in a toaster oven, microwave, or even pan fry them in a bit of oil to get 'em nice and crispy.

Walnut Chorizo Breakfast Bowl

★ **No added sugar**
★ **Quick and easy**   **Yield: 4 servings**

We don't know about you, but we're really into bowls. Breakfast is the perfect excuse to whip one up. This walnut chorizo is a breeze to throw together and requires no cooking. All of the components can be prepped ahead of time and kept in the fridge for up to a week, so it makes for a super-simple assemble-and-heat breakfast on rushed mornings. If you need a breakfast on the go, you can roll it up inside a big tortilla for a tasty breakfast burrito. The salt and added oil are totally optional here, and if the idea of tequila at breakfast time (it's only 2 tablespoons [30 ml]!) makes you squirm, simply replace it with more vinegar.

FOR THE WALNUT CHORIZO:

2 cups (240 g) walnut pieces

2 tablespoons (30 ml) red wine vinegar

2 tablespoons (30 ml) tequila

2 tablespoons (30 ml) mild-flavored vegetable oil, or vegetable broth

1 chipotle pepper in adobo sauce

1 tablespoon (8 g) minced garlic

1 tablespoon (8 g) chili powder

1 tablespoon (8 g) onion powder

1 tablespoon (8 g) ground paprika

½ teaspoon dried oregano

½ teaspoon ground black pepper

½ teaspoon ground cumin

½ to 1 teaspoon sea salt, optional

FOR THE BOWL:

1 tablespoon (15 ml) oil, optional

1 block (12 ounces, or 340 g) extra- or super-firm tofu, drained, pressed, and chopped into tiny cubes

1 can (15 ounces, or 425 g) black or pinto beans, rinsed and drained

2 cups (60 g) chopped greens, such as kale, chard, or spinach

To make the walnut chorizo: Add all chorizo ingredients to a food processor and pulse until combined and mashed. (You don't want a paste; you do want a few bigger pieces left.) Warm when ready to use.

To make the bowl: Preheat a nonstick skillet or add the oil to a skillet over medium-high heat.

Add tofu and pan fry until lightly browned. Add beans and toss to cook until warmed through. Stir in greens and cook until wilted down and warmed all the way through. Add warmed chorizo to the top. Serve immediately.

···

VEGGIE BITE

Wanna kick it up a notch? Top the bowl with guacamole, salsa, fresh cilantro, some nondairy sour cream, or your favorite shredded vegan cheese! The chorizo also makes a great filling for tacos and burritos and a topping for nachos.

···

Hearty Chik'n Noodle Soup

* Nut free
* No added sugar

Yield: 4 to 6 servings

What's more comforting than chik'n soup? It's warm and hearty and tastes amazing on a cold winter day, and especially when you aren't feeling your best. We originally wrote this recipe using all dried spices, because most people have these on hand in the spice rack. However, fresh almost always tastes better than dried, so feel free to use either.

6 cups (1.41 L) low-sodium vegetable broth

2 tablespoons (30 ml) olive oil, optional

1 tablespoon (2 g) dried parsley flakes or 3 tablespoons (6 g) fresh chopped parsley

1 tablespoon (2 g) dried chives or 3 tablespoons (6 g) fresh chopped chives

1 teaspoon onion powder

1 teaspoon dried minced onion or ¼ cup (40 g) fresh chopped onions

1 teaspoon dried minced garlic or 1 tablespoon (8 g) fresh minced garlic

½ teaspoon smoked paprika

½ teaspoon dried thyme

½ cup (96 g) dry red lentils, uncooked

½ pound (225 g) linguine noodles, uncooked and broken in half, or any pasta

1 block (12 to 16 ounces, or 340 to 454 g) extra- or super-firm tofu, drained and pressed, cut into tiny cubes (See "Veggie Bite" at right.)

Salt, to taste

Ground black pepper, to taste

In a soup pot with a tightly fitting lid, add broth and oil, if using. Add parsley, chives, onion powder, onion, garlic, paprika, and thyme. Bring to a boil.

Stir in lentils, noodles, and tofu. Reduce heat to a simmer, cover, and simmer for 10 to 12 minutes, or until pasta and lentils are tender. Season with salt and pepper to taste. Serve hot.

....

VEGGIE BITES

Instead of the tofu, you can also use chopped seitan, chopped faux chicken (such as Beyond Meat or Gardein), large-chunk textured vegetable protein, or Soy Curls.

Also, peas, carrots, and celery make fabulous additions to this already robust soup.

....

Soups and Stews

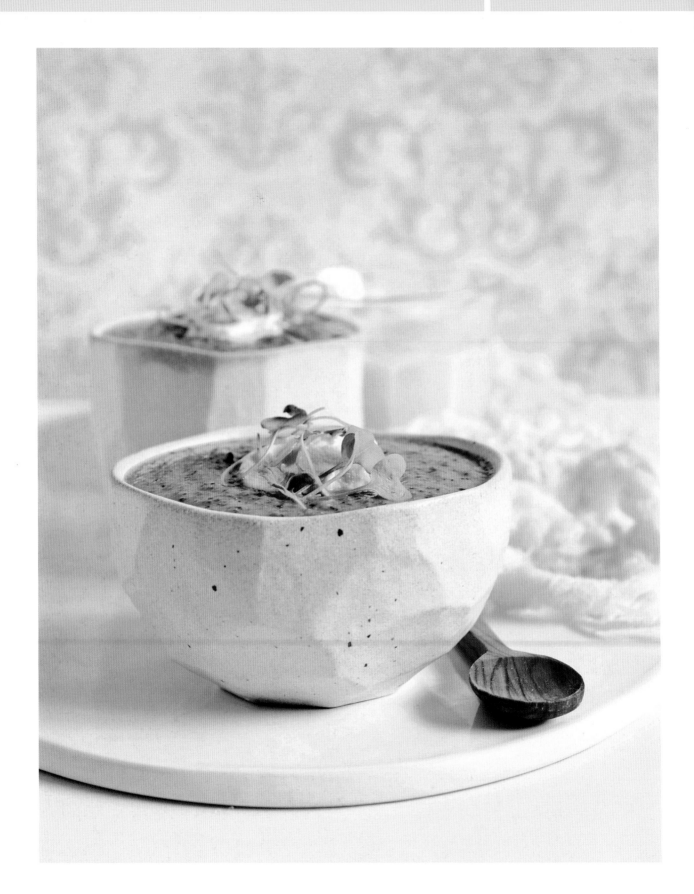

Surprisingly Good Green Soup

* Soy free
* Gluten free
* Nut free
* No added oil
* No added salt
* No added sugar

Yield: About 6 cups (1.4 L)

Most people are afraid of green food. However, this soup will change the way people view "green." This soup is delicious, and it's also a bowl full of vitamins, minerals, phytonutrients, and taste!

1 cup (160 g) chopped white onion

1 large (1 cup, or 89 g) leek, diced

3 tablespoons (40 ml) water or vegetable broth, optional

3 carrots, peeled and diced, to make 1 cup (108 g)

4 small green zucchini, chopped with skins on, to make 1 cup (113 g)

8 ounces (72 g) brown button mushrooms, chopped

1 head broccoli rabe, chopped, to make 1 cup (40 g)

1¼ cups (295 ml) carrot juice

⅔ cup (160 ml) celery juice (See "Veggie Bite" at right.)

2 cups (470 ml) low-sodium vegetable broth

Ground black pepper, to taste

1 teaspoon ground cumin

1 teaspoon turmeric

½ cup (96 g) dry lentils, uncooked

½ cup (96 g) dry split peas, uncooked

1 small bunch (1 cup, or 67 g) lacinato (Dino) kale, destemmed and cut into strips

1 small bunch (1 cup, or 36 g) collard greens, cut into strips

1 small bunch (1 cup, or 36 g) Swiss chard, cut into strips

Cashew Cream (See recipe on page 144.) or nutritional yeast, to taste

In a large pot, place onion and leek and cook over high heat until they become translucent, for about 5 minutes.

If onions and leeks begin to stick to pot, add water or broth, if using. Add carrots, zucchini and mushrooms and continue to cook over high heat until they begin to create liquid, about 7 minutes. Add broccoli rabe and cook for 5 minutes.

Decrease heat to medium and add carrot juice, celery juice, veggie broth, pepper to taste, cumin, and turmeric.

When juices and broth start to boil, add lentils and split peas. Stir and cook until the lentils and peas are soft, 20 to 45 minutes, depending on amount of heat and brand of lentils and peas. Add kale, collard greens, and chard and continue cooking until greens are cooked down, about 7 to 10 minutes.

Using a handheld mixer, purée soup until creamy or pour small batches in blender and blend until creamy. Top with Cashew Cream or nutritional yeast.

....

VEGGIE BITE

You can make your own celery juice with a juicer or buy it at a juice bar. Or you can substitute 1 cup (120 g) diced celery.

....

New England-Can-Kiss-My-Clam Chowder

* Soy free
* Nut free
* No added oil
* No added salt
* No added sugar

Yield: About 8 cups (1.9 L)

Get ready for weird, folks. Joni was so excited when putting this recipe together. She came up with the idea when she was making the Tu-Not Salad (see page 112). While the jackfruit was boiling in the broth and seaweed, she kept thinking, it smells like clam chowder! So here is her very strange—and very tasty—clam chowder, complete with seitan clams! This is a time-consuming recipe, about 2 hours, but a lot of that is down time, and it only uses one pot and one small bowl, so not too many dishes. Are you brave enough to try it?

8 cups (1.9 L) low-sodium vegetable broth

1 ounce (28 g) dried seaweed (See "Veggie Bites" at right.)

Cheesecloth

2 cups (470 ml) water

1 cup (235 ml) canned coconut milk

2 pounds (908 g) potatoes, peeled (optional) and cut into bite-sized cubes

1 cup (160 g) diced white or yellow onion

1 cup (144 g) vital wheat gluten

1 teaspoon ground black pepper

Pour broth into a soup pot with a tightly fitting lid.

Loosely tie seaweed in a satchel made from cheesecloth and place in pot with broth. Bring to a boil, reduce to a simmer, cover, and simmer for 30 minutes. Remove ½ cup (120 ml) of broth and set aside to cool. Simmer remaining broth for 30 minutes. Add water, coconut milk, potatoes, and onion. Cover and continue to simmer for 1 hour.

Meanwhile, make your clams. In a small bowl, add vital wheat gluten, pepper, and reserved ½ cup (120 ml) broth. Work with your fingers until a nice dough ball is formed. Let the dough ball rest for 5 minutes. Using a non-serrated knife, cut the dough into a gazillion little pieces.

Add dough pieces to the broth, stirring to make sure they are not all clumped together. Cover and simmer for the remainder of the hour. (At this point, there should be about 30 minutes left.) Return after 15 minutes to give it a good stir and prevent the "clams" from getting stuck to the bottom.

Remove soup from heat and remove lid. Using a wooden spoon or a hand masher, break up potatoes to thicken the soup. (Don't worry about smashing the "clams"; they are pretty unsmashable.)

....

VEGGIE BITES

If you use a very low-sodium broth, you may need to add a little salt to taste. If you are like us, a nice squirt of Tabasco or sriracha always hits the spot in clam chowder. You can also make this soup gluten free by subbing king oyster mushrooms for the seitan clams!

When choosing dried seaweed, you can use hijiki, wakame, kombu, dulse, kelp—anything but nori, because nori will dissolve into a gelatinous mess. The soup's volume will vary, depending on the type of seaweed you use.

....

Broccoli Potato "Cheese" Soup

* Soy free
* Gluten free
* Nut free
* No added sugar

Yield: 12 servings

2 tablespoons (30 ml) mild-flavored vegetable oil, optional

1 cup (160 g) diced yellow onion

1 cup (101 g) chopped celery

1 tablespoon (8 g) minced garlic

2½ pounds (908 g) red potatoes, skin on, cubed

8 ounces (227 g) fresh or frozen broccoli florets

½ cup (60 g) nutritional yeast

1 teaspoon dried parsley

½ teaspoon dried thyme

½ teaspoon dried oregano

¼ teaspoon dried coriander

¼ teaspoon turmeric

2 quarts (1.9 L) water

Salt, to taste

Ground black pepper, to taste

This soup is hearty and flavorful, without being heavy. And there's no cheese in this cheesy soup, rather some nutritional yeast and a touch of color from turmeric. The recipe makes enough for a crowd, so it's a perfect meal to make on a Sunday afternoon and enjoy throughout the week as quick heat-and-serve lunches and dinners.

In a large soup pot with a lid, heat oil (if using) over medium-high heat. Add onion and celery and sauté or dry-cook, stirring constantly until fragrant and translucent, about 5 minutes. Add garlic and continue to cook 2 to 3 minutes.

Add potatoes, broccoli, nutritional yeast, parsley, thyme, oregano, coriander, and turmeric. Toss to coat and cook 2 to 3 minutes.

Pour in water and give a good stir to mix it all up. Bring to a boil, then reduce to a simmer. Cover and simmer 45 minutes, stirring every 15 minutes.

Remove from heat. Using an immersion stick blender, purée until smooth or carefully transfer to a blender and purée in batches.

Curry, Coconut, and Carrot Blender Soup

* Soy free
* Gluten free
* Nut free
* No added oil
* No added salt
* No added sugar
* Quick and easy

Yield: 5 cups (1.2 L)

Alright, kids, it doesn't get any easier than this! Throw it all in the blender, and you're done! Heat it up whenever you want a bowl of soup. Pack in individual serving containers for easy meals at home, work, or school! As written, it has no added salt. If you use very low-sodium vegetable broth, you may need to add a little pinch of salt to your serving. For an extra smooth soup, you can opt to steam the carrots until soft before adding them to the blender.

1 can (14 ounces, or 398 g) full-fat coconut milk

2 cups (470 ml) low-sodium vegetable broth

3 cups (324 g) shredded carrots (you don't have to shred carrots if you have a very powerful blender)

1 tablespoon (8 g) minced garlic

2 teaspoons yellow curry powder

Healthy squirt of sriracha sauce, to taste

Place all ingredients in a blender and purée until very smooth.

To serve, simply heat in a pot on the stovetop or in a bowl in the microwave. To make easy-to-go lunches, pack in microwave-safe glass jars.

Miso Soup

* Gluten free
* Nut free
* No added oil
* No added sugar

Yield: About 4 cups (940 ml)

Miso soup is the most popular soup in Japan. It's one of the most nutrient-dense soups also, with seaweed as one of the main ingredients. Different misos vary in saltiness, so adjust the amount of miso to your preference.

FOR THE KOMBU (KELP) BROTH (DASHI):

½ ounce (15 g) dried kombu, unrinsed

4 cups (1 quart, or 940 ml) room temperature water

FOR THE MISO SOUP:

3 cups (705 ml) dashi soup broth

1 package (2.1 ounces, or 60 g) Wakame seaweed

1 block (12 ounces, or 340 g) firm tofu, cut into small cubes

3 to 4 tablespoons (50 to 64 g) miso paste

¼ cup (40 g) chopped green onion

To make the broth: In a cooking pot, place kombu in water. Soak 2 hours. After 2 hours, bring mixture to a boil over medium heat. Boil 2 minutes. Using a strainer, remove kombu, reserving dashi soup stock for the soup. (The kombu can be reused in other recipes. For example, place a sheet of kombu in beans when cooking them to cut down on "gas").

To make the soup: Put dashi broth in a pot over high heat. Bring to a boil. Add seaweed and tofu. Reduce heat to low. Simmer 1 to 2 minutes.

Remove ¼ cup (60 ml) soup stock from the pot and place it in a bowl. Dissolve miso into stock. Gradually return miso mixture to soup. Stir soup gently. (Try not to boil the soup after you put miso in.) When soup is heated through, remove from heat. Add onion.

VEGGIE BITE

You can use shiitake mushroom in place of kombu if you prefer. Use ½ cup (4 ounces, or 114 g) of dried shiitake mushrooms to 4 cups (1 quart, or 940 ml) of room temperature water and let soak for 30 minutes. Bring mushrooms and water to a boil and boil for 2 minutes. Remove mushrooms with strainer, and you now have a shiitake dashi. You can use the reconstituted mushrooms in other recipes calling for mushrooms.

Simple-to-Make Veggie Chili

* Soy free
* Gluten free
* Nut free
* No added oil
* No added salt
* No added sugar

Yield: 6 servings

This chili is very simple, but very good. If you're serving people who are a little vegan phobic, add the soy meat substitute or some minced, reconstituted dried shiitake mushrooms. If you're serving everyday vegans and want to go a little less processed, just leave out the soy meat substitute. This chili is soy free if made without the meat substitute, and it's gluten free if you use meat substitute that doesn't contain wheat. Enjoy!

2 cups (320 g) minced yellow or sweet onion

2 cloves garlic, minced, or 1 tablespoon (8 g) granulated garlic

3 tablespoons (40 ml) vegetable broth or water, optional

1 green bell pepper, seeded and chopped

1 red bell pepper, seeded and chopped

1 yellow or orange bell pepper, seeded and chopped

15 ounces (392 g) vegetarian meat substitute, pan-cooked, optional

1 ounce (28 g) dried shiitake mushrooms, soaked in water and then minced, optional

26 ounces (750 g) aseptically packaged tomatoes or tomatoes, chopped, with juice

1 can (15 ounces, or 425 g) kidney beans, drained and rinsed, or 1¾ cups (437 g) prepared kidney beans

1 can (15 ounces, or 425 g) black beans, drained and rinsed, or 1¾ cups (441 g) prepared black beans

2 teaspoons chili powder

½ teaspoon ground cumin

½ teaspoon ground nutmeg

½ teaspoon turmeric

Pinch ground black pepper

2 cups (470 ml) low-sodium vegetable broth

1 to 2 cups (120 g to 240 g) nutritional yeast

Tiny pinch sea salt or dried minced seaweed

Heat a deep pot over medium heat. Add onion and garlic. Cook, stirring occasionally, 6 to 7 minutes, or until onions are translucent. If onion starts to stick to pan, add broth or water. Add bell peppers and cook until they become soft, 5 to 7 minutes. Add meat substitute, if using, and mushrooms, if using. Cook 5 minutes, or until moisture starts to come out of mushrooms and meat substitute and collects in bottom of pot. Add tomatoes, kidney beans, black beans, chili powder, cumin, nutmeg, turmeric, black pepper, and broth.

Decrease heat to low. Cover pot and cook on low at least 1 hour, preferably 2 or more hours. Check occasionally and add water or vegetable broth to desired thickness.

When cooked halfway through, add nutritional yeast, in small amounts, tasting as you go. Stir. Add salt or seaweed.

....

VEGGIE BITE

Serve this chili the way you like your favorite chili. This is also exceptionally good over baked potatoes or baked sweet potatoes for a complete meal.

....

One-Pot-Meal Soup

* Soy free
* Gluten free
* Nut free
* No added oil
* No added salt
* No added sugar

Yield: 4 servings

One of the easiest and quickest ways to make dinner is to do it all in one dish.

1 onion, chopped

2 cloves garlic, minced

1 quart (4 cups, or 940 ml) low-sodium vegetable broth, divided

1 small red bell pepper, seeded and chopped

1 small yellow bell pepper, seeded and chopped

3 large carrots, peeled and chopped

2 large sweet potatoes, peeled and chopped

1 package (8 ounces, or 227 g) white or cremini mushrooms, sliced

½ cup (96 g) uncooked dry red lentils

½ teaspoon minced fresh ginger

½ teaspoon ground black pepper

½ teaspoon ground cumin

½ teaspoon chili powder

½ teaspoon ground paprika

5 ounces (140 g) baby spinach or destemmed kale, chopped

Heat a heavy-bottomed pot with tightly fitting lid over medium-high heat. Add onion and garlic. Cook until onion becomes soft or start to brown on bottom of pan. Pour about ⅛ cup (30 ml) of vegetable broth into pan. Add bell peppers and carrots.

Once peppers and carrots start to soften, add potatoes and cook, about 3 minutes. Add mushrooms and cook until mushrooms begin to soften and water from mushrooms and other vegetables starts to increase in pan, about 5 minutes.

Stir in lentils, ginger, black pepper, cumin, chili powder, paprika, and remainder of vegetable broth. Increase the heat to high. Bring the soup to a boil, then reduce heat to medium-low, cover, and simmer until lentils and vegetables start to soften, about 20 minutes. Add the greens and cook until wilted, about 10 minutes.

VEGGIE BITE

Waiting as long as you can to add the vegetable broth, instead using the moisture from the vegetables to allow the veggies to cook, will give you a soup that is very flavorful.

Taboo-Li

* Soy free
* Nut free
* No added sugar

Yield: 16 side dish servings

2 cups (470 ml) water

1 cup (140 g) fine bulgur wheat

2 bunches (about 3 cups, or 180 g) fresh parsley, finely chopped

6 Roma tomatoes, cored, seeded, and diced (about 3 cups chopped, or 540 g)

2 tablespoons (17 g) minced garlic

1 yellow onion, finely diced

¼ cup (60 ml) olive oil

2 tablespoons (30 ml) lemon juice

Salt, to taste

Ground black pepper, to taste

Tabouli, tabbouleh, tabouleh, or tambouli: It seems like each and every culture that makes it claims theirs is the most authentic. So, without any claims to being the most authentic, this version may be a little bit taboo—hence, the name. But it's fresh, light, and tasty on its own stuffed into a pita with Falafelogs (See the recipe on page 108), or over a bed of greens with garbanzo beans tossed in for a tasty Mediterranean meal. It also makes a welcoming addition to any mezze platter alongside hummus and pita.

In a large pot with a lid over high heat, bring water to a boil. Add wheat, stir, cover, remove from heat, and let stand 10 minutes. Uncover, fluff with a fork, and set aside to cool.

In a large mixing bowl, combine remaining ingredients. Add cooled bulgur wheat and toss to mix. Serve chilled.

Italian "Sausage" and Peppers Pasta Salad

* No added sugar

Yield: 16 servings

1 pound (454 g) pasta (any)

4 Italian "Sausages" (see page 124), sliced into ¼-inch (6 mm) rounds

1 green bell pepper, seeded and diced

1 red bell pepper, seeded and diced

½ cup (80 g) diced white onion

½ cup (80 g) diced red onion

½ ounce (14 g) fresh parsley, finely chopped (about ½ cup)

¼ cup (30 g) toasted pine nuts or slivered almonds

1 cup (235 ml) Tofu Mayo (see page 139)

2 tablespoons (30 ml) balsamic vinegar

½ teaspoon garlic powder

½ teaspoon dried basil

Salt, to taste

Ground black pepper, to taste

This is a great dish to bring to a potluck, especially because it makes a huge bowl. If you want to make it to have at home, feel free to halve the recipe—or even quarter it. This recipe uses four of the Italian Sausages from the recipe on page 124. That recipe makes eight sausages, so you can use the leftovers for this salad.

Prepare pasta according to package instructions. Drain pasta and let it cool.

In a large bowl, add pasta, sausages, bell peppers, onion, parsley, and pine nuts or almonds. Toss to mix.

In a small bowl, mix together Tofu Mayo, balsamic vinegar, garlic powder, and basil. Season to taste with salt and black pepper. Add dressing to salad and toss to coat. Refrigerate until ready to serve.

Salads and Sandwiches

Make a Salad a Meal

* Soy free
* Gluten free
* No added oils
* No added salt
* No added sugar
* Quick and easy

Yield:
Variable servings

Salads should always be delicious and loaded with nutrients! We've made it super easy for you to whip up a fantastic salad in no time, by spelling it all out in this recipe. Incorporate the suggested number of items from each of the categories. Select different items each time for a totally different, nutritious, and delicious salad every day. This salad is *huge!* It's meant to be eaten as an entire family meal. Incorporate the ingredients as listed below and you will have a salad that weighs well over 1 pound (454 g)!

Greens: Select 2 or 3, 1 to 2 cups chopped raw per person: arugula, Belgium endive, bok choy, butter lettuce, chicory, Chinese cabbage, collard greens, escarole, kale, mache, dandelion greens, mustard greens, radicchio, spinach, Swiss chard, Romaine, red leaf, turnip greens, watercress, or other leafy greens

Vegetables: Select 4 to 5, 1 cup raw or ½ cup cooked per person: snow peas, snap peas, green beans, cucumbers, leeks, eggplant, mushrooms, green onions, bell peppers, zucchini, tomato, cauliflower, corn, sprouts, celery, radishes, jicama, beets, artichoke hearts, okra, broccoli, carrots, cabbage, or sundried tomatoes

Beans/legumes: Select 1, ¼ to ½ cup per person: black beans, garbanzo beans, black-eyed peas, pinto beans, green peas, edamame, azuki beans, cannelloni beans, lima beans, white beans, or lentils

Grains: Select 1 or 2, ½ cup cooked per person: amaranth, millet, buckwheat, rye, quinoa, sorghum, kamut, spelt, wild rice, brown rice, barley, or teff

Fruit: Select 1 or 2, ½ cup per person: apples, berries, grapes, currants, oranges, avocado, tangerines, pears, cherries, star fruit, dates, figs, or cranberries

Nuts/seeds: Select 1, ¼ cup per person: (Ideally these should be raw, with no salt and oils added.) walnuts, pecans, almonds, cashews, coconut, ground flax seeds, pine nuts, chia seeds, sunflower seeds, or pumpkin seeds

In a large bowl, combine the selected ingredients.

....

VEGGIE BITES

Because you have so many of these textures and flavors in the salad, you don't need a fatty salad dressing for flavor. Simply add balsamic (could use a flavored one) and/or rice vinegar and seasonings, such as turmeric, curry, or cumin. Seasonings add taste and nutrition at the same time.

The amount of vinegars and seasoning depends on how many people you are serving. Vinegars = equal parts of each (½ cup for 1 to 2 people). Seasonings can be to taste (approximately ½ teaspoon per person). You can also add a little Dijon mustard to give it a little zip.

Fresh squeezed fruit juices also make a great dressing!

....

"No One Will Know It's Vegan" Potato Salad

* Gluten free
* No added oil
* No added salt
* No added sugar

Yield: 10 to 12 servings

We love, love, love potato salad, but obviously we don't eat mayonnaise. So Gerrie headed into the kitchen and came up with this delicious and filling recipe. If you don't tell your family, they won't even know it's vegan!

3 (2½ pounds, or 1.14 kg) red potatoes with the skin on, cut into ¼-inch (6 mm) cubes

3 (2½ pounds, or 1.14 kg) Yukon gold potatoes with the skin on, cut into ¼-inch (6 mm) cubes

3 (2½ pounds, or 1.14 kg) russet potatoes with the skin on, cut into ¼-inch (6 mm) cubes

⅓ cup (43 g) capers

1 can (4 ounces, or 112 g) low-sodium black olives, chopped (about 1 cup)

1 cup (160 g) diced onion, white or yellow

1 cup (101 g) diced celery

1 red bell pepper, seeded and diced

1 tablespoon (9 g) minced garlic (about 3 cloves)

2 tablespoons (6 g) dried dill

16 ounces (284 g) frozen peas, thawed

1 tablespoon (2 g) ground black pepper

4 containers (24 ounces, or 681 g) unsweetened plain soy or almond yogurt

3 tablespoons (45 g) Dijon mustard

Boil or steam potatoes until firmly cooked, but not mushy. Drain and place potatoes in a large bowl. Add remaining ingredients except yogurt and mustard.

Next add half of the yogurt and mix. Continue to add yogurt and mix until it reaches your desired creaminess. (Some people like it moister than others.) Add the mustard, mix, and taste. You may add more mustard, depending on taste.

Chill at least 2 hours before serving.

VEGGIE BITES

You can add more dill or pepper or a tiny bit of salt, to your taste.

To help the flavors meld, make this salad the day before and let it chill overnight. This salad is so delicious, it won't be around long. But it will keep for 4 days in the fridge. Enjoy this colorful, low-calorie, delicious dish!

Super Stacked Veggie "Burger"

* Nut free
* No added oil
* No added sugar

Yield: 4 "burgers"

FOR MARINADE:

⅓ cup (80 ml) coconut aminos, low-sodium soy sauce, or Bragg's Liquid Aminos

2 tablespoons (30 ml) balsamic vinegar

1 tablespoon (7 g) smoked paprika

2 teaspoons ground black pepper

1 teaspoon garlic powder

1 teaspoon onion powder

1 teaspoon chipotle powder or cayenne pepper

½ teaspoon dried oregano

½ teaspoon dried thyme

About ½ cup water (120 ml)

FOR "BURGER":

1 medium sweet onion, cut into round slices

4 medium Portobello mushrooms, brushed clean

3 medium zucchinis, sliced lengthwise in ¼-inch- (6 mm) thick slices

1 large red bell pepper, sliced lengthwise

1 medium eggplant, sliced in ¼-inch (6 mm) round slices

FOR TOPPINGS:

1 large heirloom or beefsteak tomato, sliced

2 large avocados, sliced in quarters or 1 cup guacamole

1 head Romaine lettuce, washed, dried, and pulled into separate pieces

4 hamburger buns (100 percent whole- or sprouted-grain, or your favorite gluten-free bread)

1 tablespoon (11 g) condiment, such as German mustard or ketchup

This isn't your usual burger. It's even better! Grill up extra veggies to save and use for other meals during the week. Even Gerrie's non-veggie-loving friends have asked for this recipe! Prepare for the best "burger" ever. The challenge is how to get it in your mouth!

To make the marinade: Combine all marinade ingredients in a bowl and stir. Taste test, and if it is too salty, add more seasonings until the taste appeals to your taste buds. This marinade is very concentrated, so add approximately ½ cup (120 ml) water to thin out.

To make the "burgers:" To the marinade, add onion, mushrooms, zucchinis, red pepper, and eggplant. Toss until vegetables are covered, but don't leave in marinade beyond 2 minutes.

Preheat grill. Grill vegetables on barbeque or indoor grill until soft.

Assemble sandwich in this order: bottom of bun, portabella mushroom, slice eggplant, leaf lettuce, slice tomato, 2 or 3 slices zucchini, 2 slices red bell pepper, onion, and sliced avocado or guacamole. Spread condiments on bun top, and place atop vegetables.

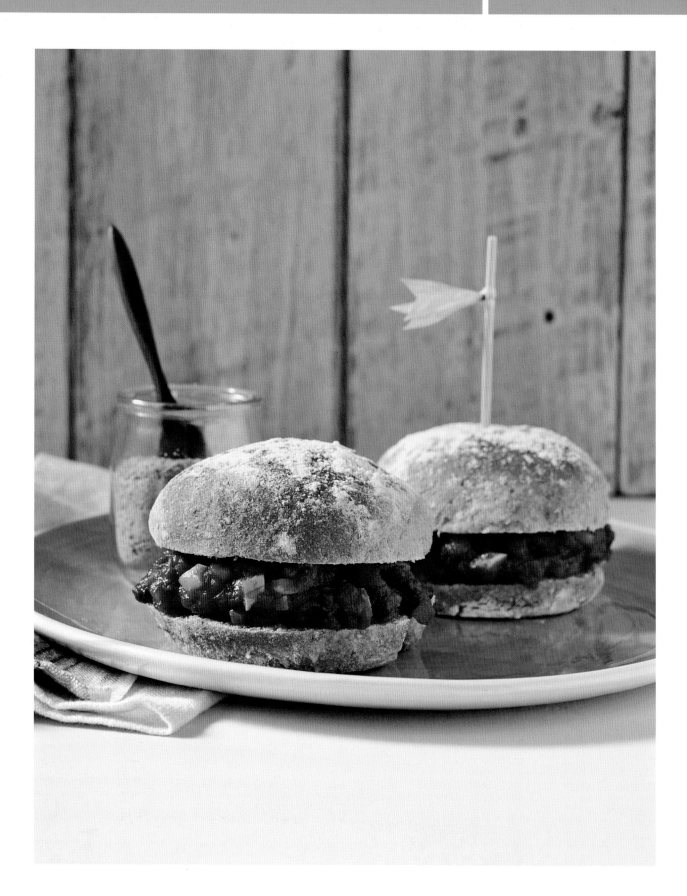

Summer Squash Veggie Sloppy Joes

* Nut free
* No added oil
* No added salt
* No added sugar
* Quick and easy

Yield: 6 sandwiches

Who doesn't like sloppy joes? This is definitely one of those dishes that you think you will never be able to have again once you go to a plant-based way of eating. Well, this recipe will convince you that this thought couldn't be further from the truth! Make your sloppy joes soy free by using beans in place of tofu. You can go gluten free by using gluten-free bread or rice tortillas instead of the hamburger buns.

1 cup (160 g) diced yellow or white onion

¼ cup (60 ml) low-sodium vegetable broth

½ cup (54 g) chopped carrot

1 cup (101 g) chopped celery

12 ounces (340 g) extra-firm tofu, drained and mashed up, or 1 can (15 ounces, or 425 g) black or pinto beans

1½ cups (170 g) peeled and chopped summer squash (zucchini or yellow squash)

6 ounces (170 g) tomato paste

3 cups (705 ml) tomato sauce or 1 package (26 ounces, 750 g) Pomi chopped tomatoes

3 cloves garlic, minced

1 teaspoon chili powder

1 teaspoon ground paprika

1 teaspoon dried oregano

1 teaspoon ground black pepper

1½ cups (355 ml) water

6 hamburger buns (100 percent whole wheat or Ezekiel Sprouted Grain buns), toasted

1 cup (120 g) nutritional yeast

In a large sauté pan over medium heat, sauté onion, adding broth once onion starts to caramelize and turn brown. Add carrot and celery and cook, stirring occasionally, 2 minutes. Add tofu or beans and summer squash, mixing well. Cook 2 minutes. Add tomato paste and sauce or tomatoes, stirring to dissolve completely. Add garlic, chili powder, paprika, oregano, and pepper. Mix until thoroughly combined.

Reduce heat to medium-low, add water, and continue to cook until mixture is thickened, stirring occasionally, 8 to 10 minutes.

Once mixture is thickened, place your desired amount of mixture on each bun, top with nutritional yeast, and *enjoy!*

Falafelogs with Cucumber Relish

* Soy free
* Nut free
* No added oil
* No added sugar

Yield: 6 to 8 servings

FOR FALAFELOGS:

1 can (15 ounces, or 425 g) chickpeas, drained and rinsed, or 1¾ cups (420 g) cooked chickpeas

1 cup (160 g) diced yellow onion (about ½ large onion)

1 Roma tomato, roughly chopped (about ⅓ cup)

1 ounce (28 g) fresh parsley (about 1 cup [5 g] fresh leaves)

½ ounce (14 g) fresh cilantro (about ⅓ cup [5 g] fresh leaves)

2 to 4 large garlic cloves, to taste

½ cup (60 g) chickpea flour

½ cup (72 g) vital wheat gluten flour

1 tablespoon (15 ml) lemon juice

1 teaspoon salt, or to taste

1 teaspoon baking powder

1 teaspoon ground cumin

¼ teaspoon cayenne pepper

FOR CUCUMBER RELISH:

½ cup (128 g) tahini (See "Veggie Bites" at right.)

¼ cup (60 ml) lemon juice

3 to 4 large cloves garlic, to taste

2 teaspoons dried dill or 2 tablespoons (7 g) fresh dill

1 medium cucumber, seeded and diced (about 1½ cups, or [205 g])

2 Roma tomatoes, seeded and diced (about ⅔ cup, or [120 g])

1 tablespoon (1 g) fresh chopped cilantro

1 tablespoon (1 g) fresh chopped parsley

Salt, to taste

Ground black pepper, to taste

6 to 8 pitas

This dish is like a falafel hot dog! These logs are fun to make, and they're easy, too! The parsley and cilantro add a bright, fresh flavor.

To make the falafelogs: Add all log ingredients to a food processor and process until a loose dough forms. (It should be the consistency of peanut butter.)

Transfer mixture to a bowl, cover, and chill 20 to 30 minutes in the refrigerator. (This step allows the gluten to develop.)

Preheat oven to 350°F (180°C, or gas mark 4). Line a rimmed baking sheet with parchment paper or reusable silicone baking mat.

Scoop about ⅓ cup (3½ ounces, or 100 g) dough and form into a log shape about 6 to 7 inches long by 1½ inches wide (15 to 17 cm long × 4 cm wide). (The dough is very soft, and you may need to form the log right on the baking sheet. Don't worry, they will firm up when baked.)

Repeat until all of the dough is used. Bake 20 minutes, flip, and bake 20 minutes, or until exterior is firm and browned. (They might look dry, but the inside will be nice and soft.)

Meanwhile, prepare the Cucumber Relish.

To make the relish: Pour tahini, lemon juice, and garlic into a blender. Purée until smooth. (The lemon juice will curdle the tahini (similar to buttermilk), resulting in an airy, fluffy mixture.)

Remove mixture from the blender and place in a mixing bowl. Fold in dill, cucumber, tomatoes, cilantro, and parsley. Season to taste with salt and pepper. Chill until ready to serve.

Assemble the pitas by placing the falafelog in the center and topping with a liberal amount of relish.

VEGGIE BITES

Tahinis vary in texture and thickness, from very liquidy to very thick. This measure assumes you're using a more liquid tahini. If yours is very thick, you may need to thin it out with water or vegetable broth to reach the consistency of a pourable milkshake. You want a total of ½ cup (120 ml), so adjust tahini amount as needed.

You can make the logs gluten free by substituting chickpea flour for the vital wheat gluten flour. The logs may be a little more fragile, but they will still taste great!

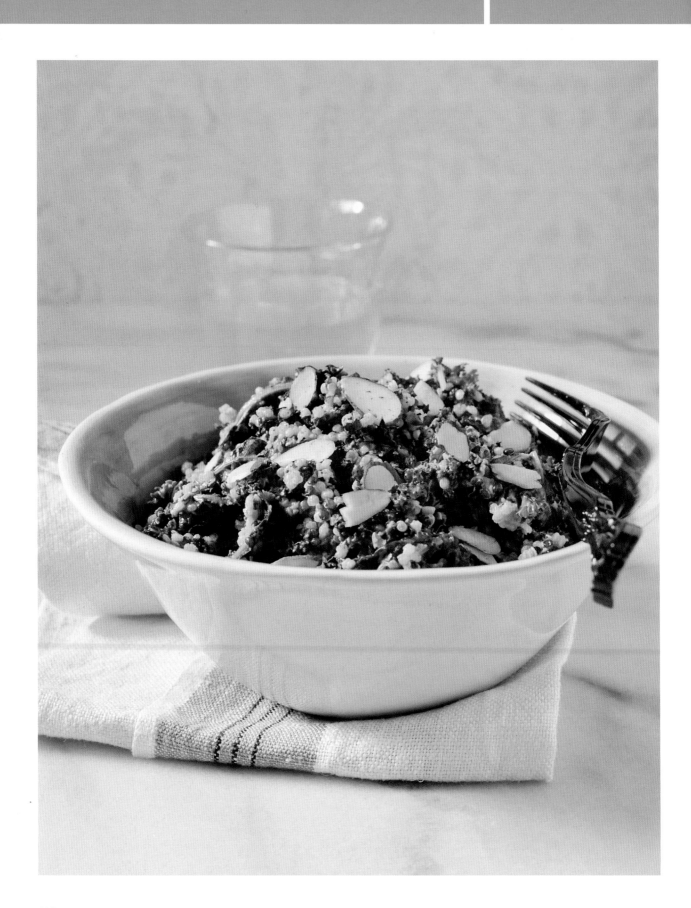

Red and White Quinoa Kale Salad

* No added oil
* No added salt
* No added sugar

Yield: 8 side dish servings

The tahini in the dressing for this salad gives it a nice rich flavor, while the raisins add an unexpected sweetness. This salad tastes great warm or cold, which makes it the perfect dish to bring to potlucks or pack for lunches.

1 cup (168 g) white quinoa, uncooked

½ cup (84 g) red quinoa, uncooked

3 cups (705 ml) water or low-sodium vegetable broth

8 ounces (227 g) chopped curly or lacinto kale

½ cup (45 g) sliced or slivered almonds (toasted or raw)

½ cup (80 g) raisins

½ cup (128 g) tahini (See "Veggie Bites" at right.)

2 tablespoons (30 ml) soy sauce, tamari, or Bragg Liquid Aminos

2 tablespoons (30 ml) lemon juice

1 tablespoon (10 g) minced garlic

In a fine mesh strainer, rinse quinoa. Strain out as much excess water as possible. (If you buy prewashed quinoa, you can omit this step.)

Place quinoa in a dry pot with a lid, and heat over medium heat to lightly toast the quinoa, stirring constantly to prevent burning, about 4 to 5 minutes.

Add water or vegetable broth, raise the heat and bring to boil. Immediately lower heat to low, cover, and cook 15 minutes. Remove from heat and allow to stand, covered, 5 minutes. Uncover and fluff with a fork.

While quinoa is cooking, blanch kale. Bring a pot of water to boil, drop in kale, give it a quick stir and then quickly remove it and place into an ice water bath to stop the cooking.

Once quinoa is cooked, place it in a mixing bowl, along with kale, almonds, and raisins.

In a small bowl, whisk together tahini, soy sauce, lemon juice, and garlic. Toss the dressing with the salad to coat. Serve immediately or refrigerate.

....

VEGGIE BITES

Tahinis vary in texture and thickness, from very liquidy to very thick. The measure in this recipe assumes that you're using a more liquid tahini. If yours is very thick, you may need to thin it out with water or vegetable broth to reach the consistency of a pourable milkshake.

If you have a rice cooker, use it to prepare the quinoa. Use a 2-to-1 ratio of liquid to quinoa and follow the instructions on your rice cooker.

....

Tu-Not Salad

This stuff is so realistic that when Joni first tasted it, it gave her that mouthwatering jaw clench she used to get when she ate tuna right out of the can with crackers. (Well, bear with her, it's probably been more than ten years since Joni has had real tuna!) Jackfruit makes an amazing stand-in for flaky tuna in this salad, and the hijiki seaweed gives it an amazingly seafood-y flavor. The recipe takes a few hours to make, but most of it is down-time, and once the jackfruit is cooked, it comes together in just a few minutes.

4 cups (940 ml) low-sodium vegetable broth

1 can (20 ounces, or 570 g) young green jackfruit, packed in water or brine, drained and rinsed (10 ounces, or 285 g, dry weight)

¼ cup (20 g) hijiki seaweed (See "Veggie Bites" at right.)

½ cup (80 g) finely diced red onion

½ cup (50 g) finely diced celery

½ cup (52 g) finely diced cucumber

2 tablespoons (8 g) finely chopped fresh parsley or 2 teaspoons dried parsley

1½ teaspoons fresh dill or ½ teaspoon dried dill

½ cup (112 g) Tofu Mayo (See recipe on page 139.)

In a large pot with a tightly fitting lid, place broth, jackfruit, and hijiki. Bring to boil over medium-high heat. Reduce to simmer, cover, and simmer 2 hours, stirring about every 30 minutes. Remove from heat, remove lid, and allow to cool to room temperature.

Drain excess liquid (reserve this flavorful stock for other uses!) and place cooked jackfruit and hijiki in a mixing bowl. Using your hands or the edge of a wooden spoon, break apart jackfruit until stringy and flaky. Add onion, celery, cucumber, parsley, dill, and Tofu Mayo. Mix until well combined.

Store in the refrigerator in an airtight container for up to 1 week or freeze for up to 4 months.

....

VEGGIE BITES

This salad tastes great on a sandwich (Hello, tuna melt on grilled sourdough with a slice of Daiya Swiss style slices!), in a wrap, on a bed of greens, or all on its own as a side dish. Add sunflower seeds for added crunch or dried cranberries, currants, or raisins for a sweet bite.

Although occasional use of hijiki is not likely to cause any adverse health concerns, many people avoid it because it may contain higher levels of dietary arsenic than is found in other seaweeds. If this is a concern, you can use wakame or kombu in this recipe. We don't recommend nori because it tends to completely dissolve.

When using seaweed other than hijiki, you'll need to strain out the seaweed after boiling. The best way to do this is to tie up the seaweed in a piece of cheesecloth before adding it to the broth, which will allow for the flavor to still be absorbed by the jackfruit, while also allowing for the seaweed to be easily removed from the broth after boiling.

....

Spinach and Artichoke Dip

* Gluten free
* Nut free
* No added oil

Yield: 8 servings

This recipe is for all of you who are now dairy free and crave that yummy spinach and artichoke dip we have all had at parties. This recipe will satisfy your desire for a creamy, delicious dip. It will not disappoint.

1 yellow onion, diced

4 cloves garlic, divided

8 ounces (227 g) marinated artichoke hearts

½ cup (120 ml) low-sodium, no-oil vegetable broth, divided

12 ounces (340 g) frozen chopped spinach, thawed, drained, and squeezed dry

1 block (12 ounces, or 340 g) firm silken tofu

¾ cup (90 g) nutritional yeast

¼ cup (60 ml) apple cider vinegar

2 teaspoons dried basil

2 teaspoons dried parsley

½ teaspoon cayenne pepper

Pinch salt

½ teaspoon ground black pepper

Preheat oven to 350°F (180°C, or gas mark 4).

Heat a sauté pan over medium heat. Add onion and two garlic cloves to pan and cook until onion becomes translucent, approximately 5 minutes. Add artichoke hearts and half the broth and sauté 3 minutes. Add spinach and cook 3 minutes, or until heated through.

Place tofu, nutritional yeast, remainder of garlic, broth, vinegar, and spices in a blender. Blend until smooth.

In large bowl, fold in spinach sauté with blender ingredients until well blended. Taste and add extra seasonings and nutritional yeast if desired.

Smooth mixture into nonstick baking dish. Bake 15 to 20 minutes, or until lightly browned on top. Serve warm.

....

VEGGIE BITE

This dip is delicious with bread or baked, no-oil tortilla chips.

....

Gerrie's Favorite Popcorn Snack

* Gluten free
* Nut free
* No added oil
* No added sugar
* Quick and easy

Yield: 4 to 6 servings

This recipe makes a great low-calorie snack that offers lots of B vitamins and other nutrients. How nice it is to have a delicious, nutritious, and low-calorie, guilt-free snack.

½ cup (100 g) unpopped popcorn kernels or unpopped organic microwave popcorn

5 to 6 squirts Bragg's Liquid Aminos in the spray bottle, or to taste, or low-sodium tamari

¼ cup (30 g) nutritional yeast, or to taste

Air-pop or microwave popcorn. After corn is popped, spray lightly with Bragg's Liquid Aminos, sprinkle with nutritional yeast, and serve!

Herb-Crusted Coconut "Chevre"

* Soy free
* Gluten free
* Nut free

Yield: 2 pounds (908 g)

Trust us here. It really does work! The mild flavor and smooth texture of coconut flour lends itself nicely to this "cheese." It also makes it suitable for people with nut allergies. You can shape this cheese in many ways—as a log, large wheel, mini logs (perfect for gifting!), blocks, or pretty much any way you want.

1 ounce (28 g) agar flakes or powder

3 cups (705 ml) water

2 cups (224 g) coconut flour

¼ cup (30 g) nutritional yeast

2 teaspoons fine sea salt

1 teaspoon onion powder

1 teaspoon garlic powder

3 tablespoons (45 ml) lemon juice

2 tablespoons (30 ml) mild-flavored vegetable oil

1 teaspoon Dijon mustard

Assorted dried herbs and spices for crust (See "Veggie Bites" at right.)

In a medium pot, place agar in water over high heat. Bring to full boil. Boil 5 minutes, whisking frequently.

In a medium mixing bowl, whisk together coconut flour, nutritional yeast, salt, onion powder, and garlic powder.

Into the boiling mixture, stir lemon juice, oil, and mustard.

Add dry mixture into the water-agar mixture and mix until well combined and resembling play-dough.

Remove from heat. Allow to cool enough to handle, but still warm and pliable. Form into desired shapes and coat with herbs and spices. Wrap with waxed or parchment paper or store in an airtight container and refrigerate overnight. (The mixture will harden into a semi-firm "cheese" that's perfect for crackers.) It will last 1 week in the refrigerator and up to 4 months in the freezer.

··

VEGGIE BITES

Here are some of Joni's favorite herb-and-spice suggestions for this recipe.

* Add 1 teaspoon of liquid smoke to the entire batch at the same time as the mustard. Coat with BBQ dry rub.

* Paprika, chipotle, parsley, garlic powder, and smoked salt

* Parsley, sage, rosemary, and thyme

* Garlic, lemon pepper, basil

* Freshly ground black pepper

* Smashed nuts

··

Snacks and Sides

Herb-Roasted Potatoes

* No added sugar
* Nut free

Yield: 4 servings

Normally, we advocate using fresh herbs whenever possible, but this recipe makes great use of dried herbs that almost everyone has on hand in the spice rack.

2 pounds (908 g) Yukon gold potatoes

2 tablespoons (12 g) low-sodium vegetable broth powder

1 teaspoon granulated garlic

1 teaspoon granulated onion

1 teaspoon dried rosemary

1 teaspoon dried thyme

1 teaspoon dried marjoram

1 teaspoon dried oregano

1 teaspoon dried dill

½ teaspoon ground paprika

2 tablespoons (30 ml) olive oil, optional

Salt, to taste

Ground black pepper, to taste

Preheat oven to 425°F (220°C, or gas mark 7).

Line baking sheet with parchment paper or reusable nonstick baking mat.

Cut potatoes into bite-size chunks and rinse in cold water. Drain and place in mixing bowl.

In a small bowl, mix together vegetable broth powder, garlic, onion, rosemary, thyme, marjoram, oregano, dill, and paprika. Set aside.

Add oil, if using, to the potatoes and toss to coat. Add spice mixture to potatoes and toss to coat.

Arrange potatoes in a single layer on baking sheet and roast 20 minutes. Toss and return to oven for an additional 10 minutes, or until lightly browned and tender.

Season to taste with salt and pepper.

Roasted Veggies

* No added oil
* No added sugar
* No added salt
* Wheat free
* Nut free

Yield: 6-8 servings

This is a great "batch" recipe. Double this recipe to have enough veggies on hand all week long. You can make five or more recipes (like veggie tacos, veggie pasta, veggie salad, veggie and rice burritos...) out of these vegetables simply by adding a couple of items and never have to clean and cook vegetables during the busy week.

2 medium white, sweet, or yellow onions, peeled and cut into quarters

4 medium zucchinis, washed and cut into 4-inch (10 cm) cubes

2 medium eggplants, cleaned and cut into 4-inch (10 cm) cubes

1 green, 1 yellow, and 1 red bell pepper, cleaned, seeded and quartered

1 tablespoon (8 g) garlic powder (or fresh crushed garlic)

1 cup (235 ml) balsamic vinegar

1 tablespoon (15 ml) Bragg's Liquid Aminos, or Coconut Aminos

Preheat oven to 350°F (180°C, or gas mark 4).

Prepare the veggies as indicated above and place in large bowl. Add balsamic vinegar and garlic to bowl with veggies. Toss veggies until all are lightly coated with balsamic.

Place veggies in a single layer on non-stick baking sheet or line baking pan with parchment paper.

Roast veggies, uncovered, for approximately 30 minutes or until soft. When soft, take out of the oven, cool and place in a bowl to be chopped and used as needed for other recipes.

Almond, Garlic, Lemon Spread and Dip ▶

* Soy free
* Gluten free
* Quick and easy

Yield: 1¾ cups (415 ml)

This dip is wonderful on crackers, raw veggies, and pita. It also makes a great spread for sandwiches, on crostini, mixed with chopped raw kale to make a kicky kale salad, or even as a unique dressing for a cold pasta salad. If you are following a low- to no-oil die, you can easily replace the oil with vegetable broth.

1 cup (120 g) raw almonds

4 to 6 cloves garlic, or to taste

½ cup (120 ml) olive oil

¼ cup (60 ml) mild-flavored vegetable oil, such as canola

¼ cup (60 ml) lemon juice

½ teaspoon sea salt, or to taste

½ teaspoon ground black pepper

½ teaspoon ground paprika

½ teaspoon dried dill or 1½ teaspoons fresh

½ teaspoon dried basil or 1½ teaspoons fresh

Soak the almonds overnight.

The next day, rinse almonds and place in a blender or food processor with remaining ingredients. Process until smooth, stopping occasionally to scrape down the sides of the container. This can take up to 5 minutes.

Store in an airtight container in refrigerator until ready to use.

Quick and Easy Raw Trail Mix

* Gluten free
* No added oil
* No added salt
* No added sugar

Yield: 24 (1 ounce, or 28 g) servings

Most commercial trail mixes contain oil, sugar, and candies with artificial colors added to them. It's so easy to make your own trail mix using raw or dry-roasted, unsalted nuts, seeds, and dried fruits to avoid extra calories and unhealthful ingredients. You should have all of these ingredients in your pantry, because they all can be used for many other recipes. Feel free to be creative by adding your own favorite raw, unsalted seeds and nuts or dried fruits.

½ cup (70 g) raw, sprouted, or dry-roasted almonds

½ cup (56 g) raw cashews

½ cup (86 g) dry-roasted, unsalted soy nuts

½ cup (32 g) raw unsalted pumpkin seeds (also known as pepitas)

½ cup (80 g) raisins

½ cup (64 g) raw, hulled sunflower seeds

In a large bowl, combine all ingredients. Store in an airtight container to keep fresh until eaten.

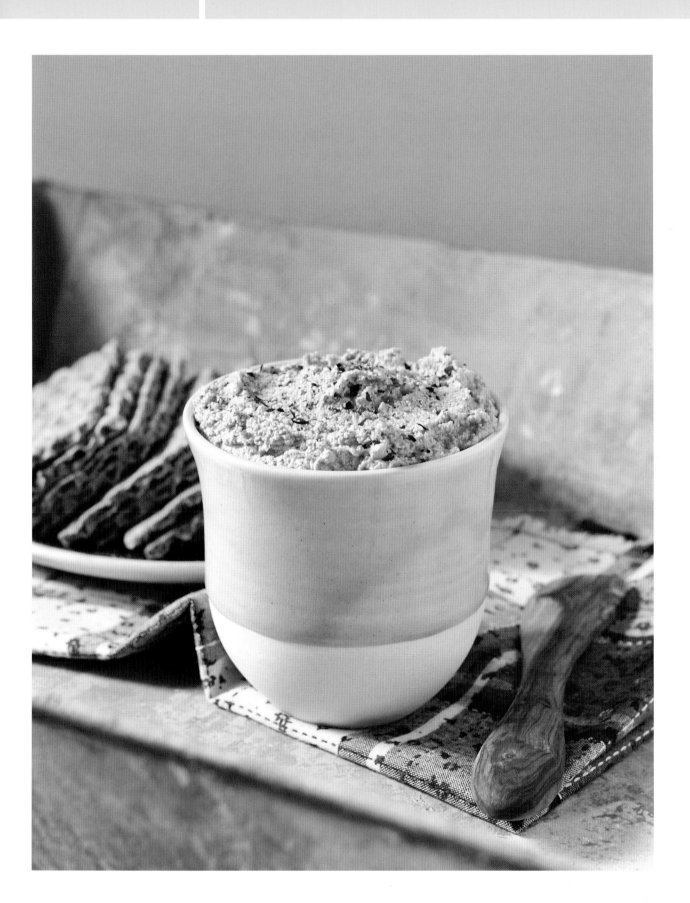

Incredibly Delicious Kale Chips

* Gluten free
* No added oil
* No added sugar

Yield: 6 to 8 servings

We either know or have heard how good kale is for us. However, most people don't know how to incorporate kale into their diets. This recipe provides a really fun and delicious way to eat more kale. Even people who would never touch kale will gobble up these delicious and nutrition-rich chips!

1½ cups (162 g) raw cashews

1 cup (235 ml) unsweetened almond milk

2 large bunches curly green or red curly kale, large stems removed, washed, and dried

½ to ¾ cup (60 to 90 g) nutritional yeast

7 to 8 squirts Bragg's Liquid Aminos or low-sodium tamari

In a bowl, cover cashews with cold water and soak at least 1 hour, preferably overnight.

Drain and rinse cashews and place in blender with almond milk. Blend to make a slightly runny paste. Add more almond milk if necessary.

Break kale into bite-size pieces and place in a large bowl. Add cashew cream to bowl. Massage the cashew coating into the kale pieces with your hands, being sure to get it inside the curls. Make sure all kale pieces are covered with cashew cream.

Place kale on dehydrator sheets. If you don't have a dehydrator, place on baking sheet lined with a piece of parchment paper.

Once kale is spread out on sheet, cover with a generous coating of nutritional yeast. Make sure each piece is covered. Pour the Bragg's Liquid Aminos into a spray bottle and lightly spray all kale chips.

If using a dehydrator, dehydrate at 145° F (63°C) for 1 to 2 hours and then lower it to 115°F (46°C) for around 8 hours, or until the coating is dry. (To be considered raw, the temperature has to stay below 118° F (48°C).)

If using an oven, preheat to 200°F (93°C), place chips in oven, and let them dry out slowly. (Keep an eye on the chips because there is a very fine line between having them dried out and burnt!) If chips are well coated, they could take 60 to 90 minutes to completely dry out.

When dried, remove from oven. Cool chips and place in airtight container. Enjoy within 3 days; after that, they will start to lose their crispness and get soggy.

Papas Rellenas

Papas Rellenas are stuffed mashed potato balls that are breaded and deep fried. Although the balls are traditionally stuffed with seasoned beef, we decided to make these balls with our Walnut Chorizo. But just because we used chorizo, there really isn't any reason you couldn't put just about anything you want to into the center of these balls. They're pretty easy and fun to make.

FOR THE BALLS:

8 russet potatoes (each about 4 inches [10 cm] long)

1 teaspoon garlic powder

1 teaspoon onion powder

¼ cup (60 ml) canola oil or other mild-flavored vegetable oil

1 cup (235 ml) almond, soy, or other nondairy milk

1 recipe Walnut Chorizo (See recipe on page 88.)

FOR THE BATTER:

Oil for frying

1 cup (80 g) panko-style bread crumbs

1 cup (125 g) all-purpose flour

1 tablespoon (2 g) dried parsley

½ teaspoon ground paprika

¼ teaspoon sea salt

¼ teaspoon ground black pepper

1 cup (235 ml) almond, soy, or other nondairy milk

To make the balls: Preheat oven to 425°F (220°C, or gas mark 7).

Line baking sheet with parchment paper and arrange cleaned potatoes on baking sheet.

Poke holes in potatoes and bake, uncovered, about 1 hour, or until fork-tender, and flesh is dry and fluffy.

Remove potatoes from oven and cut in half lengthwise. Allow to cool completely.

Once potatoes are cool, scoop out the flesh into mixing bowl. Discard skins. (Or snack on them while you are making this dish!) Add garlic powder, onion powder, and oil.

Using a hand masher, mash potatoes until well combined. Add milk a bit at a time. (The mixture should be fluffy and sticky, not wet and creamy, so add milk a little bit at a time to get the right consistency.)

Scoop ½ cup (105 g) of potato mixture into your hand and form a bowl. Place 1 heaping tablespoon (30 g) Walnut Chorizo in center. Seal potatoes around the stuffing.

To make the batter: Preheat at least 2 inches (5 cm) oil in a deep pan to 350°F (180°C). (If you have a deep fat fryer, now is a good time to use it!)

In a shallow dish, mix together panko, flour, parsley, paprika, salt, and pepper.

In a separate shallow dish, pour milk.

To prepare: Roll potato ball in milk to coat, and then into panko mix to coat. Then repeat once more. Carefully place breaded balls into hot oil, one at a time, and fry for about 30 seconds, or until golden brown and crispy. Repeat until all potato mixture is used.

VEGGIE BITE

You really can stuff anything into these balls. We love the idea of stuffing them with finely chopped seitan, peas, and Cashew Cheesy Sauce. (See recipe on page 142.) How about spinach and tofu feta? Seriously, your imagination is the only limit. You can check out a short video tutorial on making Papas Rellenas on YouTube. Search for "Vegan Papas Rellenas."

Black Bean and Roasted Veggie Tacos

* Soy free
* Gluten free
* Nut free
* No added oil
* No added sugar

Yield: 6 to 8 servings

This tasty mixture will make even the biggest of meat eaters happy! These tacos are a great way to get some of your vegetable servings in a satisfyingly filling way. Served with a side of guacamole, salsa, and a bowl of spinach, family members can assemble their tacos just the way they like them.

FOR ROASTED VEGGIES:

2 red or yellow onions, peeled and quartered

4 zucchinis, washed and cubed

2 medium eggplants, cleaned and cubed

1 green bell pepper, seeded and chopped

1 yellow bell pepper, seeded and chopped

1 red bell pepper, seeded and chopped

½ cup (120 ml) Bragg's Liquid Aminos

1 cup (235 ml) balsamic vinegar

1 tablespoon (8 g) garlic powder or 3 tablespoons fresh crushed garlic

FOR BEANS:

1 yellow onion, diced

1 tablespoon (8 g) fresh crushed garlic

1 can (15 ounces, or 425 g) no-salt-added black beans

2 cups (470 ml) low-sodium vegetable broth

YOU WILL ALSO NEED:

Guacamole

Salsa

1 bag (5 ounces, or 140 g) raw spinach

24 corn tortillas

To prepare roasted veggies: Preheat oven to 350°F (180°C, or gas mark 4). Line a baking sheet with parchment or a reusable silicone baking mat.

In a large bowl, place onions, zucchinis, eggplants, and bell peppers. Add aminos, balsamic vinegar, and garlic and toss veggies until all are lightly coated.

Place veggies on baking sheet and roast 20 minutes, or until soft. Remove from oven, cool, and chop into bite-size pieces. Place in bowl to be served.

To prepare beans: Meanwhile, heat large pot, add onion and garlic and cook until onion begins to soften. Add beans and broth and cook 10 minutes, or until heated through. After beans are cooked, purée them with a hand mixer.

To assemble: Meanwhile, in separate serving bowls, place guacamole and salsa. Chop spinach and place in serving bowl.

Use tortilla warmer or heat tortillas on stove top and place in aluminum foil to keep warm and soft. (See instructions on page 81.)

Place bowls of roasted vegetables, beans, guacamole, salsa, tortillas, and spinach on the table. Call your family to dinner and have them assemble their own tacos to their liking!

Traditional Beef-Style Simmered Seitan Loaf

* Nut free
* No added sugar

Yield: About 2 pounds (907 g)

This seitan is a great base for many recipes calling for seitan. It also tastes good when thinly sliced for sandwiches. You can also chop it and add it to stir-fries, soups, and stews.

FOR THE SIMMERING BROTH:

6 cups (1.41 L) water

½ cup (120 ml) soy sauce or tamari

¼ cup (60 ml) vegan Worcestershire sauce (No anchovies!)

2 tablespoons (16 g) garlic powder

2 tablespoons (16 g) onion powder

2 tablespoons (4 g) dried parsley

1 teaspoon ground black pepper

FOR THE SEITAN LOAF:

2 cups (288 g) vital wheat gluten flour

½ cup (60 g) whole wheat pastry flour

¼ cup (30 g) nutritional yeast

1 tablespoon (2 g) dried parsley

1 teaspoon ground black pepper

1 cup (235 ml) low-sodium vegetable broth

¼ cup (60 ml) soy sauce or tamari

2 tablespoons (30 ml) olive oil, optional, or low-sodium vegetable broth

2 tablespoons (17 g) minced garlic

YOU WILL ALSO NEED:

Cheesecloth

To make the broth: In a large pot with a tightly fitting lid, add all broth ingredients and stir to combine.

To make the seitan loaf: In a mixing bowl, stir together flours, nutritional yeast, parsley, and pepper.

In a separate small bowl, mix together broth, soy sauce or tamari, oil, if using, and garlic.

Add wet ingredients to dry and knead until a uniform, elastic dough ball is formed. Allow to rest 20 minutes before wrapping.

Form the seitan dough into a log shape about 4 inches (10 cm) in diameter. Wrap tightly with cheesecloth, wrapping several times around, and secure with knots on each end.

To assemble: Place wrapped loaf in broth and bring to boil. Reduce to simmer, cover, and simmer 2 hours, checking every 20 minutes or so, to make sure the loaf is not stuck to the bottom of the pot and flipping if necessary to make sure all sides get covered and simmered in broth.

Remove from heat and allow to cool enough to handle. Carefully remove cheesecloth, and use seitan as desired.

Store in the broth in an airtight container in the refrigerator to keep it moist. It lasts about 2 weeks in the refrigerator, or up to 4 months in the freezer.

VEGGIE BITE

Tester Claudia Desmarais gave us this tip on using the leftover simmering broth: "I like to make a gravy out of it whenever I make seitan this way. Sauté some mushrooms with onions and garlic, add some flour or fresh bread crumbs, cook until fragrant, deglaze the pan with red or white wine, then add part or all of the broth, depending on the amount of veggies/flour you used. At this point, I sometimes add fresh or dried herbs (thyme or sage, usually), lots of black pepper, additional salt, or even a bouillon cube ("beefy" flavor) if the flavor is still lacking."

Italian "Sausages"

* Nut free
* No added sugar   Yield: 8 sausages

These protein-packed wieners are juicy and full of Italian flavor. They taste great on their own or on a bun with grilled peppers, sliced or crumbled onto a pizza, or chopped and mixed into a marinara sauce to pour over pasta. (We give special thanks to Julie Hasson for her ingenious steaming method!)

1 cup (235 ml) low-sodium vegetable broth

1 block (12 ounces, or 340 g) soft silken tofu, drained and mashed with a fork

¼ cup (66 g) tomato paste

3 tablespoons (45 ml) olive oil

½ cup (80 g) finely diced white or yellow onion

½ ounce (14 g) fresh parsley, finely chopped (about ½ cup [30 g] tightly packed)

2 tablespoons (17 g) minced garlic

1 tablespoon (6 g) dried whole fennel seed

1 teaspoon dried oregano or 1½ tablespoons (6 g) finely chopped fresh oregano

1 teaspoon smoked paprika

½ teaspoon dried red chili flakes, or to taste

½ teaspoon ground black pepper

½ teaspoon dried basil or 1½ teaspoons finely chopped fresh basil

½ to 1 teaspoon salt, or to taste

¼ teaspoon cayenne pepper, or to taste

2 cups (288 g) vital wheat gluten flour

8 sheets aluminum foil measuring about 6 × 12 inches (15 × 30 cm)

In a large mixing bowl, add all ingredients, except vital wheat gluten flour. Mix until well incorporated.

Add vital wheat gluten flour and mix until a stringy dough forms. Allow dough to rest 20 minutes to allow the gluten to develop.

Divide dough into eight equal portions, about ½ cup (5 ounces, or 140 g each). Form each piece of dough into sausage shape and place near long edge of one piece of foil. Roll up foil and twist ends tight.

These can be steamed or baked. To steam, bring water in your steamer to a boil. Carefully place the wrapped sausages in steamer basket and steam 45 to 60 minutes. Remove from steamer (they should be firm to the touch) and allow to cool enough to handle.

To bake, preheat oven to 350°F (180°C, or gas mark 4). Place wrapped sausages in a single layer on baking sheet, seam side down. Bake 30 minutes, flip, and bake 30 minutes.

Remove from oven and allow to cool enough to handle. Once cooled, remove from foil and refrigerate, or freeze until ready to use.

While you can eat these right out of the steamer or oven, we have found that after they are unwrapped and cooled overnight they get nice and firm, and the flavors stand out more. To reheat, pan-fry or grill.

VEGGIE BITE

When wrapping your sausages, don't leave any extra space in the foil. Roll the foil tightly and twist the ends so it is as tight as possible. This makes the tofu cook in a confined space, forcing the sausage to be dense. To prevent blowouts, make sure the foil is wrapped around the sausage a couple of times to make it stronger.

Grilled Citrus Cauliflower "Steaks"

* Nut free
* No added salt
* No added sugar

Yield: 4 to 6 servings, depending on size of cauliflower head.

Yes, we used the word "steak" quite loosely here. But what an awesome way to announce your veganism to the world, by calling a slice of cauliflower a steak! You can grill this outside on the barbecue or indoors on a grill pan. The recipe also works well if you cut the cauliflower into florets and roast them in a single layer on a sheet pan.

FOR CAULIFLOWER "STEAKS":

1 cup (235 ml) orange juice

¼ cup (60 ml) mild-flavored vegetable oil

2 tablespoons (30 ml) lemon juice

2 tablespoons (30 ml) soy sauce or tamari

1 tablespoon (10 g) minced garlic

1 teaspoon Dijon mustard

½ teaspoon red chili flakes

Salt, to taste

Ground black pepper, to taste

1 extra-large head cauliflower

FOR CITRUS GLAZE (OPTIONAL):

Reserved marinade

2 tablespoons (16 g) cornstarch

¼ cup (60 ml) water

To make the steaks: In a shallow bowl or resealable plastic bag, whisk together orange juice, oil, lemon juice, soy sauce or tamari, garlic, mustard, and red chili flakes. Season to taste with salt and pepper.

Carefully remove stem and leaves from cauliflower. Using a sharp knife, carefully cut entire head of cauliflower into "steaks" about ½-inch to ¾-inch (1.3 to 2 cm) wide. (A large head should yield 5 or 6 steaks, with some florets left over. We call those "cutlets.")

Add steaks, and any leftover cutlets, to marinade and refrigerate overnight.

Preheat grill or grill pan to medium-high heat. Add steaks in a single layer, reserving marinade for later use as glaze, if desired.

Allow steaks to grill about 5 minutes per side, or until grill marks are prominent and cauliflower releases easily from the grill. (If it sticks too much, it isn't ready to flip.)

Flip and grill 5 minutes. Remove from grill.

To make the optional glaze: Place reserved marinade in a small pot and bring to boil. Reduce heat to simmer.

In a small bowl, mix together cornstarch and water to make slurry. Slowly pour slurry into simmering marinade and stir to thicken. Remove from heat. Glaze will continue to thicken as it cools.

Pour glaze over steak for extra-citrusy goodness.

Easy and Quick Spaghetti Squash Dish

* Soy free
* Gluten free
* Nut free
* No added oil
* No added salt

* No added sugar
* Quick and easy

Yield: 4 servings

This is probably one of the easiest and quickest dishes you'll ever make! Spaghetti squash can be used as a delicious side dish, or use it to turn your favorite pasta dish into a gluten-free delight. This is also a kid favorite, because they love to rake the spaghetti with a fork to make noodles!

1 spaghetti squash (2 to 3 pounds, or 908 g to 1.36 g)

2 cups (470 ml) pasta sauce (Super Simple Tomato Basil Pasta Sauce or Walnutty Spinach Pesto on page 141 work very well here!)

Nutritional yeast, for garnish

This dish can be baked in the oven or microwaved. To bake in the oven, preheat to 350°F (180°C, or gas mark 4). Carefully cut spaghetti squash in half lengthwise. Scoop out seeds and place squash on baking sheet or in ovenproof dish, skin side up.

Bake until soft. (Test by pressing the top skin with your finger.) A 2- to 3-pound (908 g to 1.36 g) squash will take about ½ hour. Once it's soft, remove from the oven and allow to cool slightly.

To cook in the microwave, make 4 or 5 slices around the outside of the squash. Each cut should be about 1 inch (2.5 cm) long and should enter the squash. (These slices will allow the squash to vent so that it won't explode!)

Place the pierced squash into microwave safe dish or on paper towel. (Squash will leak a little during cooking.) Microwave on high for 3-minute intervals. After each interval, turn squash. Continue cooking in this manner until squash is soft to the touch. (You don't need to make it mush, there should just be some "give" to the skin when you press on it). Small (2 to 3 pounds, or 908 g to 1.36 g) squashes will take approximately 6 minutes, depending on your microwave.

Once the squash is cooked, remove from the microwave and allow it to cool a couple of minutes. Then cut the squash in half lengthwise and remove the seeds.

Using a fork, run it along the flesh of the squash. It will peel off in little strips similar to noodles. Scrape the entire squash until you are down to the skin. Add your desired amount of sauce and toss. Top each portion with nutritional yeast.

VEGGIE BITE

The nutritional yeast makes a great garnish and makes this an incredibly yummy and vitamin-filled dish.

Roasted Sweet Potato and Sage Raviolis

* Nut free   Yield: 30 raviolis

Homemade raviolis are fun to make, and you can get the whole family involved. These freeze well, too! To freeze, place on a cookie sheet lined with parchment paper or waxed paper in a single layer and freeze until solid. Then pluck them off the sheet and store in a freezer bag.

FOR RAVIOLI DOUGH:

2 cups (334 g) semolina flour, plus additional for dusting

1 cup (235 ml) water

YOU WILL ALSO NEED:

2 dish towels

Rolling pin

Large flat surface for rolling

FOR FILLING:

2 medium sweet potatoes, peeled and cubed

2 tablespoons (30 ml) olive oil

½ teaspoon garlic powder

½ teaspoon dried sage

½ teaspoon dried thyme

Salt, to taste

Ground black pepper, to taste

Favorite pasta sauce

Note: To serve these as an appetizer, try frying them! Heat about 2 inches (5 cm) of oil in a deep pot to 350°F. (180°C) Carefully add each ravioli to the hot oil, and fry until golden and crispy—1 minute. Carefully remove from oil and place on plate lined with paper towels to absorb excess oil. Dust with a blend of garlic powder, sage, thyme, salt, and pepper. Serve warm with sauce for dipping.

To make the ravioli dough: In a mixing bowl, mix flour and water and knead into a soft but firm, elastic dough ball, about 5 minutes. Divide into four equal pieces. Leave in bowl, cover with dish towel, and allow to rest about ½ hour. After dough has rested, dust rolling surface with flour.

Flatten one piece and roll out very thin, to 1/16 of an inch (1.5 mm).

Take sheet of pasta dough and lay it on a dish towel on a flat surface. Cover with another dish towel. Repeat with remaining three pieces. (It is okay to stack pasta sheets on top of one another.) They should be pretty dry after rolling, and not too sticky. If they are too sticky, dust in between sheets with additional semolina flour.

To make the filling: Preheat oven to 375°F (190°C, or gas mark 5) and line a baking sheet with parchment paper or a silicone baking mat.

In a mixing bowl, toss sweet potatoes with oil and spices to coat. Season to taste with salt and pepper. Arrange in single layer on baking sheet.

Bake about 30 minutes, or until tender. Remove from oven and allow to cool.

Place potatoes in bowl and mash with a hand masher until a scoopable consistency is achieved. (Lumps are okay.)

To make the raviolis, lay one sheet of pasta dough on flat surface. Using a 3-inch (7.5 cm) circular cookie cutter or "pint" glass, cut as many circles as possible from the sheet. Stack the circles, reserve remaining dough. Repeat with remaining sheets. Your goal is 60 or more circles, which is enough to make 30 ravioli. If needed, you can reroll the dough remaining after cutting the circles.

Once all of your circles are cut, spoon about 1 tablespoon (15 g) filling onto the center of one circle. Top with another circle. Use the tines of a fork to seal the edges.

Bring a pot of salted water to a boil. Drop three or four raviolis into the boiling water at a time. Cook 3 to 5 minutes. Remove from water. Serve warm, topped with your favorite pasta sauce.

···

VEGGIE BITE

For these ravioli, white sauces taste much better than reds, especially the Al-Mond-Fredo Sauce. (See the recipe on page 137.)

···

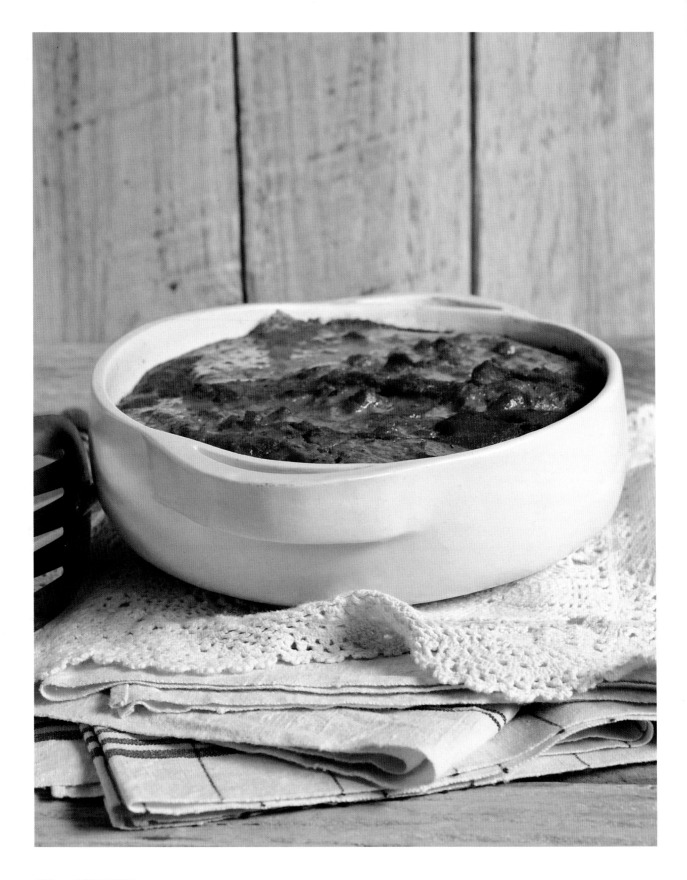

Black Bean and Summer Squash Enchiladas

* Soy free
* Gluten free
* Nut free
* No added oil
* No added sugar

Yield: 8 enchiladas

These enchiladas are a great way to get more veggies into the diet for people who don't like veggies. It's also a delicious way to enjoy enchiladas! We enjoy them baked with a little Cashew Cheesy Sauce on top. (See the recipe on page 142.)

6 ounces (170 g) tomato paste

15 ounces (434 g) tomato sauce

½ teaspoon chipotle powder, or to taste

1 cup (160 g) finely diced onion

½ cup (120 ml) low-sodium vegetable broth, optional

2 cloves garlic, minced

1 medium red bell pepper, seeded and chopped, or ½ red and ½ green bell pepper

2 medium zucchini or yellow summer squash, diced

1½ cups (378 g) black beans, well rinsed and drained

1 bunch spinach, washed and chopped, or 1 small package (5 ounces, or 140 g) washed

1½ teaspoons ground cumin

¼ teaspoon ground black pepper

⅛ teaspoon salt

2 teaspoons lime juice

8 organic corn tortillas

6 green onions, sliced, for garnish

Preheat oven to 350°F (180°C, or gas mark 4).

In a large bowl, combine tomato paste, tomato sauce, and chipotle powder and stir. (This makes a quick and easy enchilada sauce that gives you control over the "heat." This mixture can be warmed while you do the next step, or just set aside. The spiciness will increase once the total dish is baked.)

Heat large sauté pan and add onion. Cook onion until it starts to soften. If onion starts to stick to bottom of pan, add broth. When onion softens, add garlic and cook 2 minutes.

Stir in bell pepper and squash and cook, stirring occasionally, 2 to 3 minutes, or until squash becomes tender. If vegetables start to stick to bottom of pan, add broth. Once squash is tender, add beans, spinach, cumin, black pepper, and salt. Simmer 5 minutes to allow spinach to wilt. Remove from heat and stir in lime juice. Taste and add additional seasonings if desired.

Spread thin layer of tomato mixture to the bottom of a 9 × 13-inch (22 × 33 cm) ovenproof dish. Dip a tortilla in the bowl of tomato mixture until it is completely covered with tomato sauce.

Lay coated tortilla in bottom of dish. Spread large tablespoon (one-eighth) of veggie–bean mixture across center of tortilla. Gently roll up tortilla and place seam-side down in baking dish at one end. Take next tortilla, dip in the tomato mixture and repeat the remaining steps until you have all of the tortillas filled, rolled and placed next to each other in dish.

When all enchiladas are rolled, pour remaining tomato mixture over enchiladas. Cover and bake approximately 20 minutes. (The dish doesn't need to be cooked, but just thoroughly heated through.)

After 20 minutes, check to make sure dish is bubbling hot. Then remove from oven, sprinkle with green onions, and serve.

....

VEGGIE BITE

You can sprinkle some nutritional yeast on top if you love nutritional yeast. Serve these enchiladas with your favorite guacamole or salsa.

....

Tahini Noodle Bowl

Yield: 4 very hearty main dish servings

FOR SAUCE:

1 cup (235 ml) tahini

¼ cup (60 ml) soy sauce or tamari

¼ cup (60 ml) balsamic vinegar

¼ cup (60 ml) water

2 tablespoons (30 ml) sesame oil, optional

1 tablespoon (15 ml) molasses

1 tablespoon (15 ml) sriracha

1 tablespoon (8 g) garlic powder

1 teaspoon Dijon mustard

FOR BOWL:

1 pound (454 g) spaghetti or any preferred pasta

2 tablespoons (30 ml) mild-flavored vegetable oil, optional

1 block (10 to 12 ounces, or 280 to 340 g) extra- or super-firm tofu, drained and pressed, cut into tiny cubes

1 cup (108 g) shredded carrots

2 cups (270 g) chopped broccoli florets

1 cup (134 g) green peas

1 cup (170 g) shelled edamame

½ cup (145 g) cashews (raw or roasted)

½ teaspoon red chili flakes

Salt, to taste

Ground black pepper, to taste

4 cups (120 g) arugula or spinach

1 tablespoon (8 g) black or white sesame seeds

Seems like bowls are all the rage in the vegan community right now. You can make noodle bowls so many ways and serve them hot or cold. We thought this would be a fun one to share, because it shows how easily a restaurant-style dish can be made at home, plus it gives you an idea on how to create your own bowl dishes anytime. The oil is completely optional. You can replace it in the sauce with 2 extra tablespoons (30 ml) of tahini, and for the stir-fry, you can simply use vegetable broth or water in lieu of oil. If you're avoiding wheat pasta, feel free to replace the spaghetti with any variety of grains, such as quinoa, brown rice, or bulgur.

Prepare pasta according to package directions.

To make the sauce: Meanwhile, in a small bowl, place sauce ingredients. Whisk ingredients until smooth. Transfer to squeeze bottle, and set aside until ready to use.

To make the bowl: Add oil, if using, to a wok or frying pan and heat over medium high. Add tofu, carrots, broccoli, peas, edamame, cashews, and red chili flakes. Toss to combine. Season to taste with salt and pepper. Sauté 6 to 8 minutes, or until veggies are bright and vibrant and tofu is slightly browned.

To assemble the bowls: Start with four pasta-size bowls. Add one-quarter of the arugula to the bottom of the bowl. Top with one-quarter of the spaghetti. Next add one-quarter of the stir-fry mixture. Top with desired amount of sauce and sprinkle with sesame seeds to finish.

···

VEGGIE BITE

These bowls can be served hot or cold, which makes them ideal make-ahead meals and easy to pack for lunches throughout the week. Simply leave off the sauce until ready to enjoy!

···

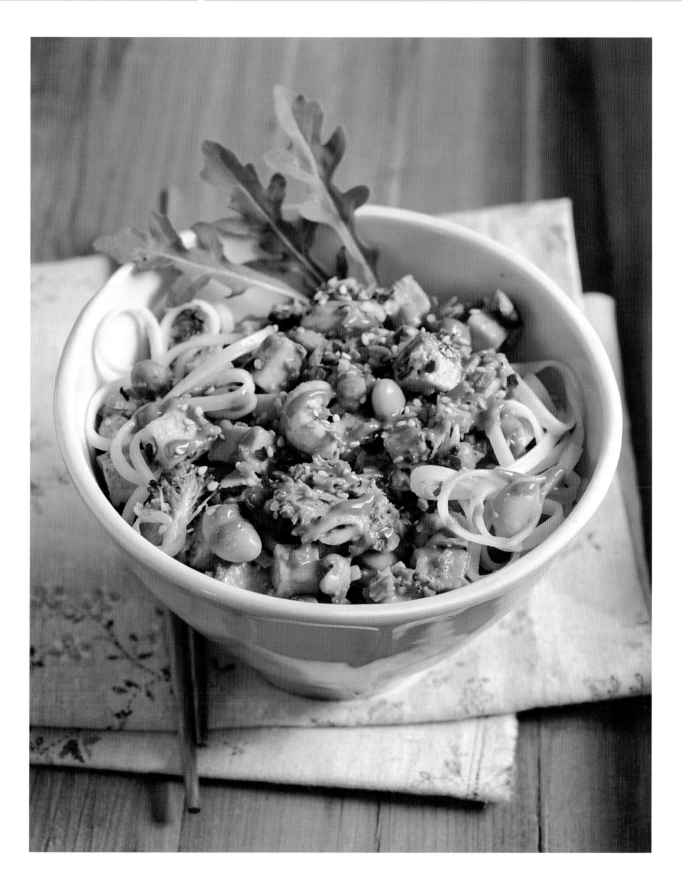

Cabbage and Onion Casserole

* Gluten free
* Nut free   Yield: 4 servings

This easy casserole is inspired by Eastern European cabbage pies. Joni lightened it by leaving off the heavy bread crust, which also makes this dish gluten free. If you're following a no-oil diet, simply leave out the oil when sautéing the onions and cabbage; just use a good nonstick pan, and add a little water if the onions start to stick. Following this traditional recipe is a gussied-up version that includes dumplings. The dumpling version is not gluten free.

2 tablespoons (30 ml) mild-flavored vegetable oil, optional

2 medium yellow onions, thin julienne cut

1 pound (454 g) green cabbage, shredded

1 tablespoon (8 g) minced garlic

1 block (14 ounces, or 396 g) soft silken tofu

¼ cup (30 g) nutritional yeast

1 tablespoon (15 g) whole grain mustard

½ teaspoon dried tarragon or 1½ teaspoons fresh chopped tarragon

¼ teaspoon ground black pepper

Sea salt, to taste

In a large frying pan, heat oil, if using, over medium-high heat. Add onions and sauté 3 to 5 minutes, or until fragrant and translucent. Add cabbage and toss. Cook 2 to 3 minutes. Add garlic and toss to mix.

Reduce heat to medium and continue to cook until reduced by half and cabbage is slightly browned, about 10 minutes, stirring often.

Preheat oven to 350°F (180°C, or gas mark 4). Have ready an 8-inch (20 cm) square baking dish.

Meanwhile, make the sauce. Place tofu, nutritional yeast, mustard, tarragon, and pepper in a blender (or use an immersion stick blender). Season to taste with salt. Puree until smooth.

Remove vegetables from heat and stir in sauce. Toss to coat completely.

Transfer mixture to baking dish and bake 45 minutes, or until top is golden brown. Remove from oven and allow to rest 10 to 15 minutes before serving.

....

VEGGIE BITE

Add very thinly sliced potatoes to the bottom of the dish, then layer cabbage filling, another layer of potatoes, and repeat, like making lasagna! Veggie add-ins that taste awesome include mushrooms, carrots, celery, and peas.

....

Dumpling, Cabbage, and Onion Casserole

* Nut free   Yield: 8 servings

Looking for some real comfort food? Try dumplings! For this version, you'll need to use a 9 × 13-inch (23 × 33 cm) baking dish.

1 recipe Cabbage and Onion Casserole (See opposite page.)

3½ cups (438 g) all-purpose flour

1 teaspoon baking powder

1 teaspoon baking soda

½ teaspoon salt

2 cups (470 ml) soy milk

2 tablespoons (30 ml) lemon juice

¼ cup (56 g) melted nondairy butter

Follow recipe for Cabbage and Onion Casserole all the way until ready to put into casserole dish.

In a large mixing bowl, combine flour, baking powder, baking soda, and salt.

In a separate small bowl, combine soy milk and lemon juice. (It will curdle and become like buttermilk.) Add melted butter to the soy milk mixture and stir to combine.

Add wet ingredients mix to dry and stir to combine. (Some lumps are okay. The batter will be wet, like a very thick pancake batter.)

Add half cabbage casserole mixture to bottom of baking dish in a single layer. Using an ice-cream scoop, carefully drop the dumplings all over the layer of cabbage. Repeat until all of the batter is used and dough balls almost create a solid layer on top of cabbage. Add remaining cabbage mixture all over and around dough balls.

Loosely cover with aluminum foil (to keep the moisture in) and bake 45 minutes, or until dough balls are fully cooked. (They will still look moist on the outside, but the insides should be fluffy.)

To serve, scoop dough balls along with some cabbage into a bowl. Serve hot.

Pizza Dough or Bread Bowls

* Nut free

A homemade pizza beats take-out any day, especially when you make your own yeast-risen dough! You can use this dough for more than just pizza, too. You can make your own hamburger buns, dinner rolls, or our favorite—bread bowls. You can also sub up to half of the all-purpose flour with whole wheat pastry flour, but this may require adding a little more water.

1 envelope (¼ ounce, or 7 g) active dry yeast

1 teaspoon granulated sugar

½ cup (120 ml) warm water

2 cups (250 g) all-purpose flour

½ cup (72 g) vital wheat gluten flour

½ teaspoon salt

½ cup (120 ml) water

1 tablespoon (15 ml) extra-virgin olive oil

2 tablespoons (30 ml) additional olive oil, for brushing

¼ cup (60 ml) melted nondairy butter or more olive oil, for brushing (bread bowls only)

In a small bowl, mix together yeast, sugar, and water. Let stand 10 minutes.

In a mixing bowl, mix together flours and salt. Add yeast mixture, second ½ cup (120 ml) water, and 1 tablespoon (15 ml) oil. If the dough is too wet, add more all-purpose flour. If the dough is too dry, add more water, a little bit at a time. (Your goal is a soft elastic dough ball that is easy to handle and not sticky.)

Knead dough about 10 minutes. Divide into two pieces and form each piece into ball. Brush with a light coat of oil, cover with plastic wrap, and let rise 1 hour.

Preheat oven to 450°F (230°C, or gas mark 8).

To make pizza dough: Punch down each dough ball, knead 2 to 3 minutes, and form into pizza crusts. Bake with your favorite toppings about 10 minutes, or until crusts are a nice golden brown.

To make bread bowls: Preheat oven to 400°F (200°C, or gas mark 6). Follow above directions up to the first rise. Punch down each dough ball, knead 2 to 3 minutes, and form into balls. Cut a few crisscross slits across the top of dough balls. Bake 15 minutes, remove from oven, brush liberally with butter or olive oil. Return to oven and bake 5 minutes, or until golden brown.

Remove from oven and let sit about 5 minutes to cool. Carefully cut a circle out of the top of each ball to create a bowl.

Al-Mond-Fredo Sauce

* No added sugar
* Quick and easy

Yield: About 1 cup
(235 ml)

This rich cream sauce tastes great on pasta. It's especially yummy on Roasted Sweet Potato and Sage Ravioli. (See page 129.) It also makes a great base for a white pizza!

½ stick (¼ cup, or 56 g) nondairy butter or ¼ cup (56 g) coconut oil

½ cup (120 ml) unsweetened soy or other nondairy milk

½ teaspoon garlic powder or 1 clove garlic, minced

Pinch ground nutmeg

¼ cup (28 g) finely ground almonds (raw or dry-roasted)

1 tablespoon (8 g) all-purpose flour

Salt, to taste

Ground black pepper, to taste

In a small saucepan, place butter or coconut oil, milk, garlic, and nutmeg. Heat on medium-low until completely melted and mixed.

Add almonds and flour. Stir vigorously to prevent any lumps. Remove from heat. (Sauce will continue to thicken as it cools.) Season to taste with salt and pepper. Serve warm.

Dijon Fig Balsamic Vinaigrette

* Nut free

Yield: Just under 2 cups (450 ml)

This sweet and tangy dressing tastes awesome on any salad. It also works well to dress steamed bitter greens, such as kale, Brussels sprouts, chard, and collards.

½ pound (227 g) or 8 fresh ripe figs

1 cup (235 ml) apple juice

¼ cup (60 ml) lemon juice

¼ cup (60 ml) balsamic vinegar

2 tablespoons (30 ml) olive oil

1 tablespoon (15 g) Dijon mustard

Trim stems off figs and halve each fig lengthwise.

In a saucepan with a tightly fitting lid, bring figs, apple juice, and lemon juice to boil. Reduce heat to simmer, cover, and cook 20 minutes.

Remove lid and continue to simmer until liquid is reduced by half, about 10 minutes, stirring often. Smash the figs with the edge of the spoon as you stir. Remove from heat and allow to cool.

Add vinegar, oil, and mustard. Transfer the mixture to a blender (or use an immersion stick blender) and purée until smooth.

Store in an airtight container in the refrigerator for up to 2 weeks.

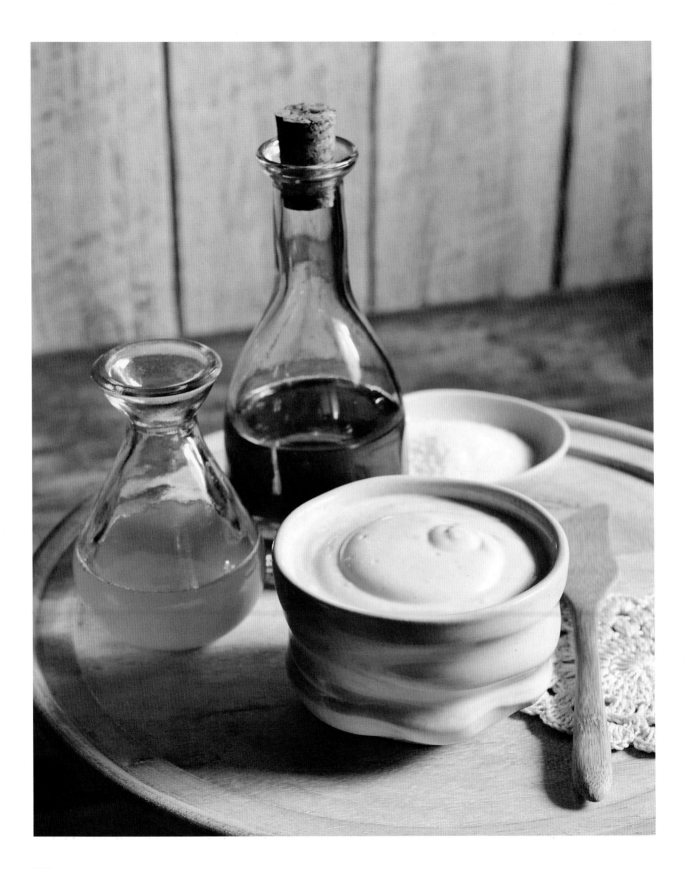

◄ Homemade Tofu Mayo

* Nut free
* Quick and easy

Yield: Just over 2 cups (475 ml)

Store-bought vegan mayo may be delicious, but not all of us have access to a health food store that carries it. Besides, it can get a bit pricey. This version is super easy and fast to make. It makes a great base for salad dressings, aiolis, and spread on a sandwich!

1 package (12 ounces, or 340 g) soft silken tofu, drained (See "Veggie Bite" at right.)

⅓ cup (80 ml) extra-virgin olive oil

⅓ cup (80 ml) canola or other mild-flavored vegetable oil

1 tablespoon (15 ml) apple cider vinegar

1 tablespoon (15 ml) lemon juice

1 tablespoon (15 g) Dijon mustard

1 tablespoon (13 g) evaporated cane juice or agave nectar

1 tablespoon (8 g) nutritional yeast, optional

½ teaspoon sea salt, or to taste

In a blender, purée ingredients until silky smooth. Transfer to an airtight container and store in the refrigerator for up to 2 weeks.

VEGGIE BITE

For dressings and sauces, use soft silken tofu. For thicker mayo, dips, and spreads, use firm silken tofu.

Walnut Parm-y Sprinkles

* Soy free
* No added oil
* No added sugar
* Quick and easy

Yield: About 1½ cups (126 g)

These simple sprinkles make an excellent topping for pasta, pizza, salads, casseroles, or just about anywhere grated Parmesan would be used.

½ cup (60 g) walnut pieces

½ cup (60 g) nutritional yeast

½ cup (40 g) panko style bread crumbs

¼ to ½ teaspoon salt, or to taste

Place all ingredients in a very dry blender or food processor and pulse to combine until walnut pieces have been ground into a powder. Store in an airtight container and refrigerate to maximize freshness. Will last at least 2 weeks in the refrigerator.

VEGGIE BITE

Spice it up! These sprinkles take well to a variety of spices. For example, to make Italian-flavored Parm-y Sprinkles, add ½ teaspoon dried basil, ¼ teaspoon fennel seed, ¼ teaspoon dried parsley, ¼ teaspoon dried oregano, and ¼ teaspoon marjoram to the mix.

Kenter Canyon Farms Greens Goddess Dressing

* Soy free
* Nut free
* No added sugar
* Quick and easy

Yield: 1½ cups (355 ml)

¾ ounce (21 g) fresh chives, chopped very fine

¾ ounce (21 g) fresh chervil (or flat-leaf parsley), chopped very fine

¾ ounce (21 g) fresh tarragon, chopped very fine

1 ripe avocado, peeled and mashed well with a fork

1 to 2 lemons, juiced and strained of seeds and pith, to taste

1 cup (235 ml) good olive oil

Salt, to taste

Ground black pepper, to taste

Joni was fortunate enough to have had the opportunity to tour the Kenter Canyon Organic Farm and meet Andrea Crawford, the owner/farmer at Kenter Canyon Farms. (See "Andrea Crawford" on page 44.) After the tour, we had lunch on the farm, and everything on our plate was grown right there! Andrea even grew the wheat that she used to bake the bread. What an amazing experience. Talk about connecting with your food! Andrea was kind enough to share her recipe for her Goddess Dressing.

In a jar with a tightly fitting lid, combine all ingredients. Shake vigorously to mix.

VEGGIE BITE

This Goddess Dressing is delicious poured over washed, dried greens as a salad dressing. Or you can use it in place of mayonnaise on a sandwich.

Super Simple Tomato Basil Pasta Sauce

* Soy free
* Nut free
* No added oil
* No added salt
* No added sugar

Yield: About 4 cups (940 ml)

½ cup (120 ml) low-sodium vegetable broth

1 cup (160 g) diced yellow or white onion

1 tablespoon (8 g) minced garlic

3 pounds (1.36 kg) ripe tomatoes, roughly chopped

10 to 15 fresh basil leaves, chopped

½ teaspoon dried oregano or 1½ teaspoons fresh oregano

¼ cup (30 g) nutritional yeast

1 tablespoon (15 ml) lemon juice

This easy sauce is the perfect accompaniment to the Easy and Quick Spaghetti Squash. (See the recipe on page 128.) Adding nutritional yeast at the end thickens it just a bit and adds a nice depth of flavor that's hard to put your finger on, unless you know it's in there.

In a large soup pot, bring broth to boil. As soon as it begins to boil, add onion and garlic. Boil, stirring often, about 5 minutes. Add tomatoes, basil, and oregano. Stir, reduce heat to medium, and simmer uncovered 1 hour, stirring occasionally. Stir in nutritional yeast and lemon juice.

Serve as is, or if desired, use an immersion stick blender (or carefully transfer to a blender) and purée to desired smoothness.

Walnutty Spinach Basil Pesto

* Soy free
* No added oil
* Quick and easy

Yield: Just over 1 cup (245 ml)

WITH OIL OPTION:

1 cup (30 g) tightly packed baby spinach

20 large basil leaves

½ cup (60 g) walnut pieces

2 tablespoons (15 g) nutritional yeast

1 clove garlic

½ cup (120 ml) olive oil

½ teaspoon lemon juice

Salt, to taste

Ground black pepper, to taste

WITHOUT OIL OPTION:

1 cup (30 g) tightly packed baby spinach

20 large basil leaves

½ cup (60 g) walnut pieces

2 tablespoons (15 g) nutritional yeast

2 cloves garlic

½ cup (120 ml) low-sodium vegetable broth

1 teaspoon lemon juice

¼ teaspoon Dijon mustard

Salt, to taste

Ground black pepper, to taste

We present this pesto recipe two ways: with and without oil. This recipe proves that oil-free can be delicious! Believe us when we say, the oil-free version tastes every bit as delicious as the oil version. Using a blender versus a food processor for this recipe gives it a really silky smooth texture, which makes this sauce perfect for so many different uses—as a spread for crostini or sandwiches, over pasta (hot or cold), as a dressing, over potatoes, as a dip, and more.

For either recipe, place all ingredients in a blender and purée until smooth. Use immediately, or transfer to an airtight container and store in the refrigerator. Use within a week, or freeze for up to 4 months.

Cashew "Cheesy" Sauce

* No added oil
* No added salt

Yield: 3 cups (705 ml)

This sauce tastes great over pasta, potatoes, vegetables, or anywhere a tasty cheesy sauce would be used. As written, this recipe has no added salt. Feel free to add salt to taste after it's prepared.

1 cup (112 g) raw cashews

2 cups (470 ml) low-sodium vegetable broth

¼ cup (30 g) nutritional yeast

¼ cup (32 g) arrowroot powder or cornstarch

2 tablespoons (34 g) tomato ketchup

1 tablespoon (10 g) minced garlic

1 tablespoon (18 g) white or yellow miso paste

1 tablespoon (8 g) onion powder

1 tablespoon (15 ml) lemon juice

1 to 2 teaspoons Dijon mustard, or to taste

½ teaspoon turmeric

½ teaspoon ground paprika

Soak cashews in water overnight. Rinse and drain.

In a blender, purée all ingredients. Purée until silky smooth.

Transfer mixture to a pot and heat over medium heat, whisking constantly, until thickened.

Use immediately, or cool and store in an airtight container in the refrigerator until ready to use. Will last up to 1 week in the refrigerator.

To reheat, warm on stovetop or in microwave, adding water or vegetable broth if needed to thin it out.

VEGGIE BITES

To make this into nacho sauce, add one whole jalapeno (or about eight slices from a jar) with or without seeds, depending on how hot you like it, and ½ teaspoon of cumin and blend. Then stir in one finely diced Roma tomato and ¼ cup (40 g) finely diced red or yellow onions.

Looking for an even easier queso? Simply stir your favorite salsa into prepared sauce.

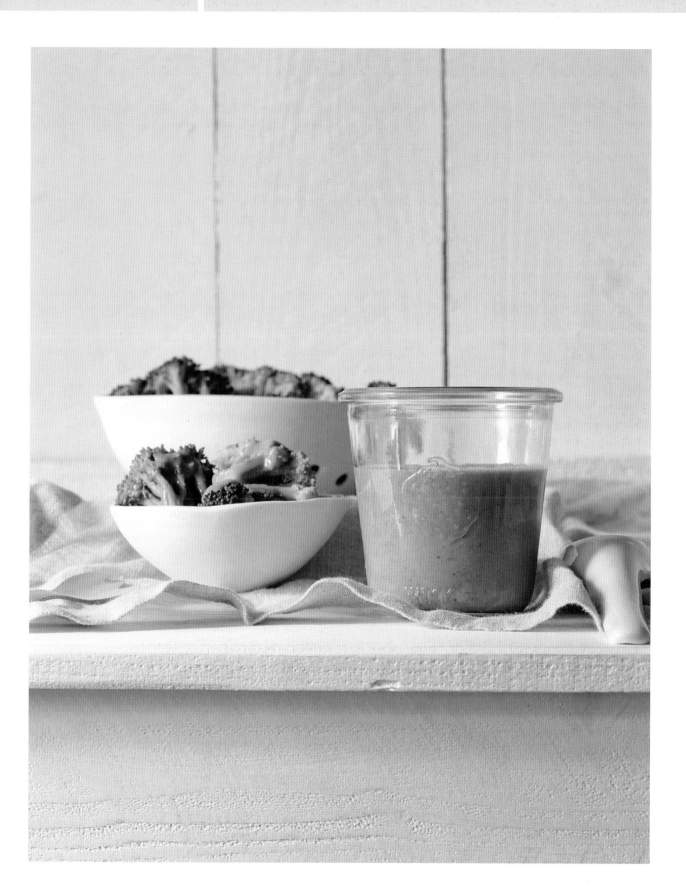

Red Wine Mushroom Gravy

* Gluten free
* Nut free
* No added oil
* No added sugar

Yield: 8 to 10 servings

1 cup (160 g) diced white onion

4 cloves garlic, finely chopped

4 ounces (114 g) cremini mushrooms, cleaned, trimmed, and chopped

4 ounces (114 g) mixed wild mushrooms, cleaned, trimmed, and chopped

2 tablespoons (4 g) chopped fresh thyme

1 tablespoon (2 g) finely chopped fresh rosemary

3 cups (705 ml) Merlot

3¼ cups (764 ml) low-sodium vegetable broth, divided

2 tablespoons (30 ml) reduced-sodium tamari

3 tablespoons (24 g) nutritional yeast

2 tablespoons (16 g) cornstarch

3 teaspoons black pepper

Add this gravy to your favorite beans and greens for a hearty combination. Or serve it over whole grains or mashed potatoes.

In large skillet over medium-high heat, add onion and garlic and cook until onion is translucent, about 4 minutes.

Stir in mushrooms, thyme, and rosemary and continue to cook about 2 minutes, or until mushrooms release their liquid and start to become tender. Add wine and cook 1 minute, stirring constantly. Stir in broth and reduce heat to simmer.

In small bowl, whisk together tamari, nutritional yeast, and cornstarch to form a thick paste. Take some hot liquid from pan and add to mixture. Stir until well mixed and there are no lumps.

Add paste to skillet, constantly and slowly whisking to make sure paste dissolves. Increase heat to bring to boil and boil 1 minute, stirring constantly. Add pepper. If gravy is too thin, whisk in flour to thicken.

Serve immediately.

Cashew Cream

* Soy free
* Gluten free
* No added oil
* No added salt
* No added sugar
* Quick and easy

Yield: 2 cups (470 ml)

Cashew cream is a versatile ingredient that can be used in sweet or savory applications. The basic recipe is simple, only two ingredients. The variations make this cream so adaptable.

2 cups (224 g) raw cashews

1 cup (235 ml) water or nondairy milk

Cover raw cashews in water and soak for at least 4 hours, up to overnight. (Or you can boil them in water for 20 minutes.)

Drain the cashews and rinse in clean water. Place cashews in a blender and add water or nondairy milk and purée until smooth. For thinner cream, use more liquid. For a thicker cream, use less.

VEGGIE BITE

For a sweet cream, add agave or other sweetener to taste. You can also add flavor extracts, such as vanilla or almond.

For a savory cream, try adding garlic and onion powders, sea salt, black pepper, or even chipotle powder.

Spiced Almond Biscotti

* Gluten free
* No added oil
* No added sugar

Yield: 10 to 12 biscotti

When Gerrie began eating healthy, crispy breads were one thing she really missed. So she decided to take a traditional biscotti recipe, and, with the help of a fabulous baker friend (thanks Gina!), she adapted this recipe into her healthy eating standards. This recipe takes a little time, but it's well worth it!

1¼ cups (150 g) almond flour

1 tablespoon (8 g) arrowroot or cornstarch

Small pinch sea salt

¼ teaspoon baking soda

½ teaspoon ground cinnamon

½ teaspoon ground ginger

Pinch ground cloves

¼ cup (50 g) date paste (See "Veggie Bite at right.)

⅓ cup (36 g) slivered almonds, pecans, walnuts, or pumpkin seeds

¼ cup (38 g) currants

Preheat oven to 350°F (180°C, or gas mark 4). Line baking sheet with parchment paper or reusable silicone baking mat.

In a food processor, combine almond flour, arrowroot or cornstarch, salt, baking soda, cinnamon, ginger and cloves. Pulse until well combined. Add date paste and pulse until dough forms ball.

Remove dough from food processor and add almonds or nuts and currants with your hands or a spoon.

On the baking sheet, form two logs from the dough. Bake 15 minutes, then remove from oven and cool 1 hour.

Remove logs to cutting board and cut into ½-inch (1.3 cm) slices on the diagonal with a very sharp knife. Place slices on baking sheet.

Lower oven heat to 300°F (150°C, or gas mark 2) and bake slices 12 to 15 minutes.

Remove from oven and let sit 20 minutes to set, cool, and become crispy.

....

VEGGIE BITE

To make your own date paste, put approximately 10 to 12 dried, pitted dates in a blender and cover with hot water. Let date-water mixture sit for 10 to 15 minutes, allowing dates to soften. Then blend into a paste.

....

Desserts

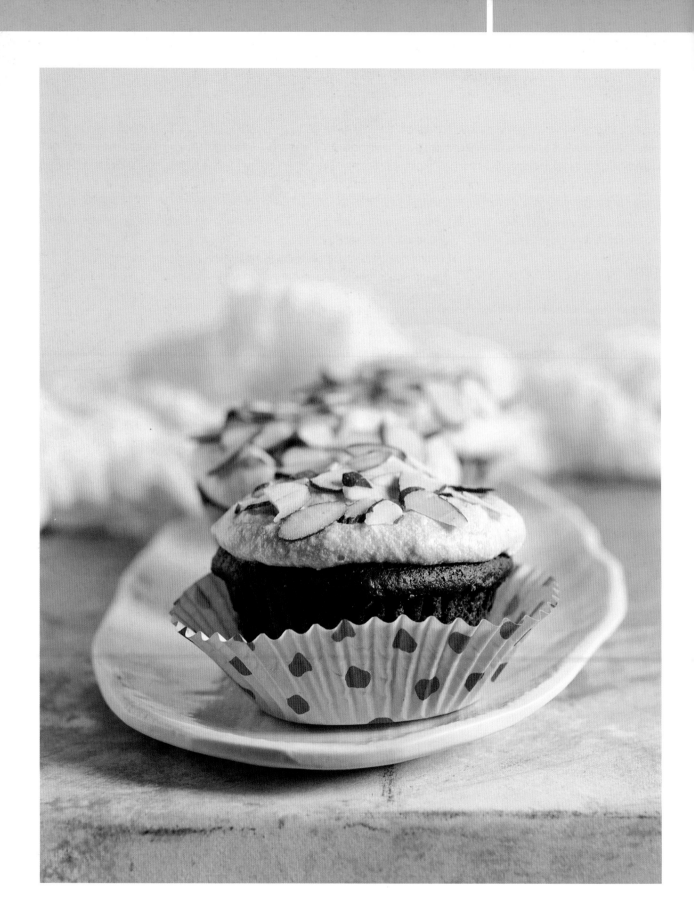

Amaretto Cupcakes

* No added oil   Yield: 12 cupcakes

There are hundreds upon hundreds of kid-friendly cupcake recipes out there. This is not one of them. This sophisticated cupcake is made for grown-ups! The cupcake itself has no added fat, so if you are watching your fat, you can make these without frosting, or try the Chocolate Ganache. (See the recipe on page 152.) For a nice decorative touch, sprinkle the tops with sliced or slivered almonds.

FOR CUPCAKES:

1 cup (235 ml) almond milk

2 tablespoons (30 ml) white vinegar

½ cup (120 ml) amaretto liqueur, such as DiSaronno (See "Veggie Bite" at right.)

1 teaspoon vanilla extract

½ cup (100 g) evaporated cane juice or vegan granulated sugar

2 cups (250 g) all-purpose flour

½ cup (40 g) unsweetened cocoa powder

1 teaspoon baking soda

½ teaspoon baking powder

½ teaspoon salt

¼ teaspoon ground cardamom

FOR FLUFFY ALMOND VANILLA FROSTING:

½ cup (112 g) nondairy butter

1 teaspoon vanilla extract

2 to 5 cups (240 to 600 g) powdered sugar, as desired

½ cup (120 ml) amaretto liqueur, such as DiSaronno (See "Veggie Bite" at right.)

To make the cupcakes: Preheat oven to 350°F (180°C, or gas mark 4). Line a standard muffin tin with cupcake papers.

In a small bowl, mix almond milk and vinegar. (It will curdle and become like buttermilk.) Stir in DiSaronno or amaretto, vanilla, and evaporated cane juice or granulated sugar.

In a large mixing bowl, sift together flour, cocoa, baking soda, baking powder, salt, and cardamom.

Add wet ingredients to dry and stir to combine. (Take care not to over mix.) Fill cupcake papers three-quarters full.

Bake on center rack 18 to 20 minutes, or until toothpick inserted in center comes out clean. Remove from oven, allow to cool enough to transfer to a cooling rack, and cool completely. (This step is important to prevent the bottoms of your cupcakes from getting soggy.) Allow to cool completely before frosting.

To make the frosting: In a mixing bowl, place butter and vanilla and beat with an electric mixer until smooth. Add powdered sugar, 1 cup (120 g) at a time until desired consistency is reached. (For a thinner icing use 2 to 3 cups [240 to 360 g]; for a fluffy, pipeable frosting use 4 to 5 cups [480 to 600 g].)

Add liqueur 1 tablespoon (15 ml) at a time as needed to taste and for desired consistency

....

VEGGIE BITE

The big square knob on top is a sure sign that this is a classic liqueur worthy of space in any well-stocked bar. However any amaretto will certainly do the trick. Joni has also offered substitutions for people who choose not to imbibe.

Teetotalers rejoice! For the amaretto in the cupcakes and frosting, substitute 1 tablespoon (15 ml) almond extract mixed with 7 tablespoons (105 ml) water or additional almond milk.

You can feel free to sub up to half of the flour with whole wheat pastry flour.

....

Tropical Fruit Cobbler

* Soy free
* Nut free

Yield: 9 servings

Instead of using the usual peaches or apples, this cobbler puts a tropical spin on a traditional favorite. You can use fresh, frozen, or canned fruit. If using frozen fruit, thaw it first and drain any excess liquid so you have 1 full cup (250 g) of thawed fruit.

1 cup (181 g) pineapple chunks

1 cup (180 g) mango chunks

1 cup (145 g) pitted cherries

½ cup (100 g) plus 3 tablespoons (38 g) evaporated cane juice or vegan cane sugar, divided

½ cup (110 g) brown sugar, tightly packed, divided

1¼ teaspoons ground cinnamon, divided

⅛ teaspoon ground nutmeg

1 teaspoon fresh lemon juice

2 teaspoons cornstarch

1 cup (125 g) all-purpose flour (See "Veggie Bite" at right.)

1 teaspoon baking powder

½ teaspoon salt

6 tablespoons (90 ml) coconut oil, chilled until solid

¼ cup (60 ml) boiling water

¼ cup (30 g) shredded coconut

Preheat oven to 425°F (220°C, or gas mark 7).

In a large bowl, combine pineapple, mango, cherries, ¼ cup (50 g) cane juice, ¼ cup (55 g) brown sugar, ¼ teaspoon cinnamon, nutmeg, lemon juice, and cornstarch. Toss to coat evenly and pour into a 9 × 9-inch (23 × 23 cm) glass baking dish or nine individual ramekins. Bake 10 minutes.

Meanwhile, make the topping. In a large bowl, combine flour, the remaining ¼ cup (50g) cane juice, the remaining ¼ cup (55 g) brown sugar, baking powder, and salt.

Using your fingers or a pastry blender, blend in oil until mixture resembles coarse meal. Stir in water until just combined.

In a separate bowl, mix together 3 tablespoons (38 g) cane juice, the remaining 1 teaspoon cinnamon, and coconut, set aside.

Remove fruit from oven, and drop spoonsful of biscuit topping over it. Sprinkle entire cobbler with the cane juice mixture. Bake until topping is golden, about 30 minutes.

....

VEGGIE BITE

You can sub half of the flour with whole wheat pastry flour.

....

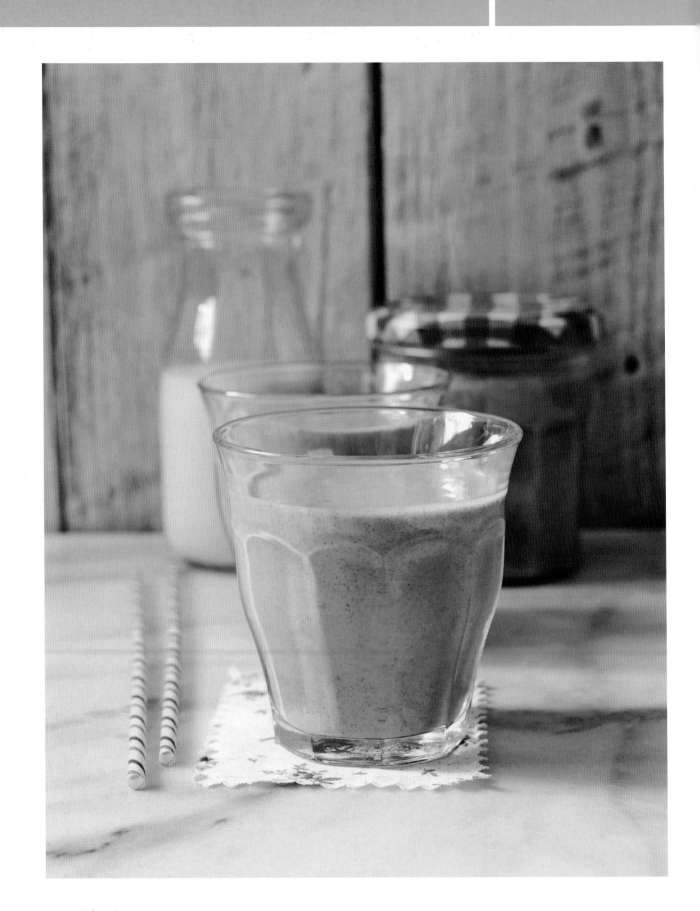

Peanut Butter and Chocolate Protein Shake

◄

* Gluten free
* No added oil
* No added salt
* No added sugar
* Quick and easy

Yield: 1 large or 2 small shakes

Gerrie came up with this delicious shake one Sunday afternoon when she had a hankering for a Reese's Peanut Butter Cup. This shakes satisfies your craving for that peanutty chocolate fix, and it's also a great way to get some good-quality protein in the most yummy way.

12 pitted dates

Hot water, as needed

½ cup (120 ml) unsweetened almond milk

2 tablespoons (32 g) creamy, no-sugar-added peanut butter

2 tablespoons (10 g) unsweetened cocoa powder

12 ounces (340 g) soft silken tofu

Handful ice cubes

In a blender, place dates and enough water to cover. Soak dates approximately 10 to 15 minutes.

When dates have softened, place milk, peanut butter, cocoa, and tofu in blender and blend until smooth. Add ice cubes at the end to make it cold.

Chocolate Pudding or Mousse

* Gluten free
* No added oil
* No added salt
* No added sugar
* Quick and easy

Yield: 4 servings

This recipe is so quick and easy it's almost unbelievable! In less than 10 minutes, you can have a delicious, nutritious, and guilt-free refrigerator dessert. This recipe will be sure to please the whole family.

¼ cup (50 g) date paste (See page 145.)

½ cup (20 g) cocoa powder

1 block (12 ounces, or 340 g) extra-firm tofu, drained (Use soft or firm if you would prefer more of a mousse than a pudding.)

¾ cup (180 ml) nondairy milk

In a blender or food processor, place all ingredients and process until smooth. Pour into a bowl, cover, and refrigerate for 1 hour or more.

VEGGIE BITE

You can pour this delicious pudding into parfait glasses or individual serving dishes and refrigerate it for mousses. You can also double the recipe and pour it into a prebaked pie shell and refrigerate. You can use cold, firm pudding in place of frosting for cakes.

Fudgy Good Frozen Treats ▶

* Gluten free
* No added oil
* No added salt
* No added sugar
* Quick and easy

Yield: 3 to 4 large
or 6 small popsicles

This delicious recipe is a variation of the Peanut Butter and Chocolate Protein Shake. (See the recipe on page 151.) The only problem you'll have with these treats is keeping them from being eaten too quickly! Because they don't last very long, you may want to double or triple this recipe.

12 pitted dates

Hot water, as needed

2 tablespoons (32 g) peanut butter

2 tablespoons (10 g) unsweetened cocoa powder

1 package (340 g) firm, silken tofu

2 teaspoons vanilla extract, optional

In blender, place dates and pour in enough water to cover. Soak dates approximately 10 to 15 minutes.

When dates have softened, add peanut butter, cocoa, and tofu in blender and blend until smooth and creamy. Pour into Popsicle molds and freeze. (If you have trouble with your blender not mixing because there is not enough liquid, add just enough milk alternative, such as unsweetened almond milk—approximately ¼ cup (60 ml)—to get the mixture to blend. If you use too much milk alternative, the treats will be icy and not creamy when frozen.) Enjoy!

Chocolate Ganache

* Soy free
* No added oil
* No added salt
* No added sugar
* Quick and easy

Yield: 2 cups (470 ml)

This is the most amazing ganache ever! By adding a little water, you can make this ganache into a chocolate sauce that no one will know is not milk chocolate! This ganache also makes a great option for the Amaretto Cupcakes. (See the recipe on page 147.)

10 pitted dates

Hot water, as needed

1 cup (256 g) creamy almond butter

2 teaspoons vanilla extract

½ cup (40 g) unsweetened cocoa powder

In a blender, place dates and pour in enough water to cover. Soak dates approximately 10 to 15 minutes.

When dates have softened, add almond butter, vanilla, and cocoa and blend until smooth and creamy.

....

VEGGIE BITE

Add ⅓ cup (80 ml) water to turn this ganache into a delicious chocolate sauce for dipping.

....

Raw Walnut Fudge

* Soy free
* Gluten free
* No added oil
* No added sugar

Yield: 20 pieces

These moist, rich, chocolatey squares may become a new favorite treat. Note that they need to be stored in the freezer to keep their shape, because the mixture is very moist.

2 cups (240 g) raw walnuts

2 cups (294 g) packed, pitted, and roughly chopped dates

½ cup plus 2 tablespoons (50 g) unsweetened cocoa powder

1 tablespoon (15 ml) pure vanilla extract

½ teaspoon sea salt

Soak walnuts in cold water 4 to 6 hours. Drain and place in food processor. Pulse until chopped. Add dates and pulse to chop, stopping frequently to scrape down sides. Add cocoa, vanilla, and salt. Process until mixture is almost smooth, scraping sides as needed to keep mixture moving. (Mixture will form a ball similar to dough, with tiny bits of walnuts remaining.)

Transfer to 8 × 8-inch (20 × 20 cm) square baking dish and press down evenly with wet fingers. Freeze 4 to 6 hours, or until well chilled.

Cut into squares. Store in freezer until ready to serve.

No-Bake Thumbprint Cookies ▶

* Soy free
* Gluten free
* No added oil
* No added sugar
* Quick and easy

Yield: About 2 dozen cookies

Gerrie made this version of these cookies, which are inspired by a Whole Foods Market recipe that was inspired by a recipe from Dr. Joel Fuhrman, author of *Eat for Health*, *Eat to Live*, and *The End of Diabetes*. They're easy to make, great for holidays, and absolutely delicious. Try a variety of different preserves each time you make them.

¾ cup (110 g) pitted dates

Hot water

3 cups (245 g) rolled oats

1½ cups (375 g) creamy almond butter or peanut butter

½ cup (40 g) shredded coconut

Zest of 1 orange

Juice of 1 orange

½ teaspoon ground cinnamon

⅛ teaspoon salt

¾ cup (240 g) cherry or apricot fruit preserves

Line a rimmed baking sheet with parchment paper or reusable silicon baking mat.

Place dates in a medium bowl. Add hot water to bowl until it just covers dates. Set bowl aside 10 to 15 minutes to let dates become soft.

Meanwhile, in a food processor or blender, pulse oats until coarsely ground. Transfer to a large bowl and set aside.

Take dates and half of the soaking liquid and place in blender. Purée until smooth. (If dates are not blending easily, add more soaking water until it blends easily.)

Add blended dates, almond butter, coconut, orange zest, orange juice, cinnamon, and salt to bowl with oats. Knead together to make a dough.

Take a small amount of dough and roll it into a ball. Place ball onto baking sheet. Continued until you have rolled all of the dough.

Make an indentation with your thumb in the middle of each dough ball to slightly flatten out the dough and leave a well in the middle. Spoon a bit of the fruit preserve into each indentation and chill at least 1 hour before serving.

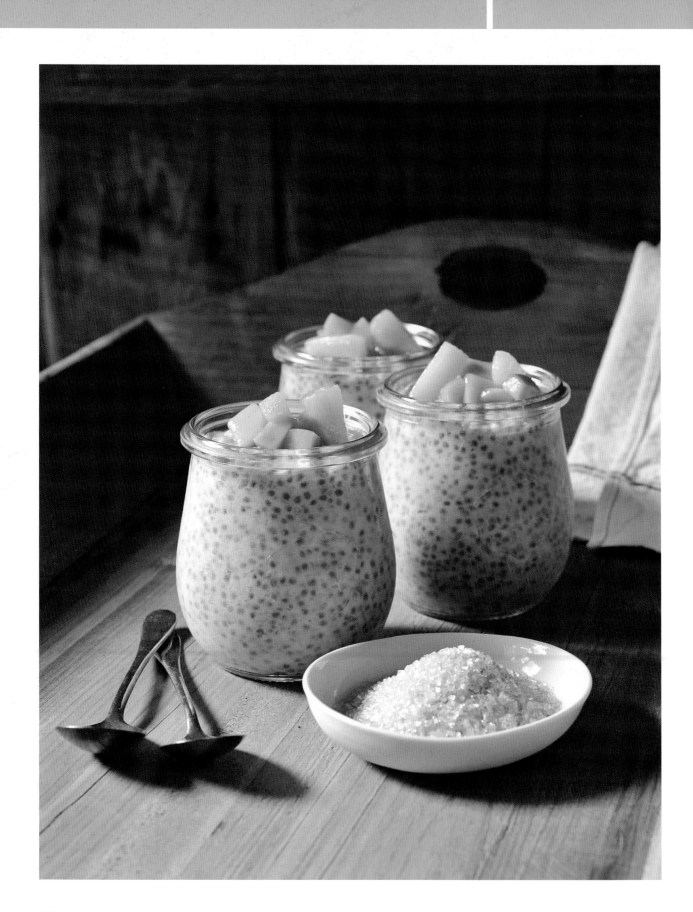

Pineapple, Mango, Coconut, and Chia Seed Pudding

◄

* Soy free
* Nut free
* No added oil
* No added salt

Yield: 8 servings

2 to 3 cups (470 to 705 ml) canned coconut milk, divided

1½ cups (280 g) frozen pineapple chunks, plus more for garnish, optional

1½ cups (280 g) frozen mango chunks, plus more for garnish, optional

2 tablespoons (30 ml) lemon juice

½ cup (60 g) shredded coconut

½ cup (120 g) chia seeds

Zest of 1 lemon

Sweetener, to taste, optional

This cool tropical treat is full of naturally sweet fruit goodness. It's also packed full of omega-3 fatty acids from the chia. We love the texture of the seeds. They remind us of tapioca pearls.

In a blender, place 2 cups (470 ml) coconut milk, pineapple, mango, and lemon juice and purée until smooth. (It should be the consistency of a thin milkshake, not too thick.)

Pour the mixture into a mixing bowl and stir in coconut, chia seeds, and zest. Cover and chill to thicken. Stir before serving. If needed, stir in extra coconut milk to achieve desired consistency. If desired, top with additional pineapple and mango chunks.

Brown Rice and Peanut Butter Treats

* Soy free
* Gluten free
* No added oil
* No added salt
* No added sugar

* Quick and easy

Yield: 8 servings (2-inch [5 cm] square pieces)

Rice crispy treats were always one of Gerrie's most favorite snacks. However, the traditional recipe is full of sugar, and it doesn't use whole grains. So Gerrie came up with her own version. This recipe is made with whole grains, and it drastically reduces the sugar without losing the flavor!

1 cup (256 g) peanut butter, at room temperature

½ cup (100 g) date paste (See page 145 to make your own.)

3 tablespoons (45 ml) agave

¼ cup (29 g) arrowroot flour

10 ounces (283 g) whole grain brown rice cereal (Gerrie uses Barbara's brand.)

In a mixing bowl, combine peanut butter, date paste, and agave. Then add flour to thicken. If mixture is too thick, transfer it to a pan and heat it on very low heat to make it a little runnier.

Mix in cereal. If mixture is cool enough to handle, mix gently with your hands until all of the rice cereal is coated and wet mixture is completely incorporated into the cereal. You can then test by taking a pinch and trying to mold it into a small ball in your hand. If the mixture sticks together you are good. If it does not, you may need to add some more date paste, rice bran, or peanut butter. Taste test to see which you would like to add. If the mixture is too hot, mix it with a spoon.

Press mixture lightly into 9 × 9-inch (23 × 23 cm) glass ovenproof dish. You may also make single servings by placing mixture into small disposable cups or molds for easy "pop-out." Make sure mixture is lightly packed down into pan. Place in refrigerator to chill and harden.

Chapter 7

Sample Menu Plans

Plans and Shopping Lists

Understanding how to do something and then actually putting it into practice are two different things, and sometimes not so simple. Even though you now have all this information on how to make that transition to a plant-based eating plan, we thought we would give you some sample menus and show you how to make sure you're eating enough and getting the correct nutrition.

Because we know that there are many reasons for choosing a path to WellBeing, we also know that there are many ways to accomplish this goal. To make this transition as easy as possible for people who are making the switch for reasons of compassion, as well as those who are trying to heal their bodies through food, we have provided you with menus for both.

Daily and Weekly Menu Plans

The first week of menus is expertly crafted with optimum nutrition and ease in mind. This menu is free of any added refined sugars, oils, and flours. It uses a lot of leftovers and easy-to-grab snacks. This menu is designed to require as little cooking as possible. It also will fill you up with nutrient-dense foods to keep you satiated, and still make sure you enjoy your food with tasty snacks and even desserts.

The second week of menus is more geared toward the transitioning vegan— someone who is nervous that they will be missing out on their favorite meaty-cheesy foods and stuck eating only "rabbit food." Fear not, this menu is filled with hearty foods that will keep you full, while satisfying the need for your favorite classic comfort foods.

MENU 1

One of our favorite practices is to "Cook once, and eat two or three times." With a little bit of preparation, you can make it easier and also less expensive to eat plant-based. For example, let's start out the week by making the roasted vegetable dish. Once this dish is made, you will have vegetables cut up, cooked, and ready for the week. By using these prepared vegetables and adding a couple of items, you can make 10 to 12 dishes during the week without having to clean, cut, and cook vegetables. Here is how you do it!

On Sunday, make the Roasted Veggies (page 117.) Use these vegetables to make different "Under 30-minute" dinners during the week. They are yummy, nutritious, easy, and cheap. It doesn't get any better than this!

Monday

Breakfast	Creamy Quinoa Breakfast Cereal (page 76) with fresh berries and cinnamon herbal tea
Mid-morning snack	Apple or your favorite piece of fresh fruit
Lunch	Make a Salad a Meal (page 100)
Mid-afternoon snack	Fresh fruit or vegetable juice
Dinner	Make a one-dish dinner, a standard pasta dish using whole grain pasta (whole wheat, brown rice, quinoa) and a no-oil pasta sauce, such as Walnutty Spinach Basil Pesto (page 141). Then add chopped, previously roasted vegetables. Serve with a green salad or simply add chopped spinach to pasta sauce. Be sure to make extra pasta for lunch the next day.
Dessert	Chocolate Pudding (page 151), make extra pudding to have on Friday.

Tuesday

Breakfast	Drink Your Greens Smoothie (page 79)
Mid-morning snack	Bowl of whole grain cereal with bananas, berries, and your favorite plant milk
Lunch	Leftover vegetable pasta
Mid-afternoon snack	1 ounce (28 g) raw, unsalted nuts or Quick and Easy Raw Trail Mix (page 118)
Dinner	Summer Squash Veggie Sloppy Joes (page 107) (save leftovers for Thursday) and a side salad
Dessert	No-Bake Thumbprint Cookies (page 154). (Save the leftovers.)

Wednesday

Breakfast	Crispy Toaster Waffles (page 73)
Mid-morning snack	Fresh fruit of choice (Choose seasonal for the most nutrients and taste.)
Lunch	Make a Salad a Meal (page 100)
Mid-afternoon snack	Incredibly Delicious Kale Chips (page 120)
Dinner	Black Bean and Roasted Veggie Tacos (page 122) , using previously roasted vegetables and serve with guacamole and oil-free, baked corn chips
Dessert	Fudgy Good Frozen Treats (page 152).

Thursday

Breakfast	Creamy Quinoa Breakfast Cereal (page 76) with cinnamon and dried fruit
Mid-morning snack	Fresh seasonal fruit
Lunch	Leftover Sloppy Joes with small side salad
Mid-afternoon snack	Dry-roasted, low-sodium soy nuts
Dinner	Simple-to-Make Veggie Chili (page 97) with side salad
Dessert	Leftover No-Bake Thumbprint Cookies

Friday

Breakfast	Your favorite breakfast smoothie
Mid-morning snack	Bowl of whole grain cereal with bananas, berries, and your favorite plant milk
Lunch	Make a Salad a Meal (page 100)
Mid-afternoon snack	Fresh seasonal fruit
Dinner	Black Bean and Summer Squash Enchiladas (page 131) (Use leftover premade roasted veggies to replace vegetables if you still have some.)
Dessert	Chocolate Pudding or Mousse (page 151)

Saturday

Breakfast	Drink Your Greens Smoothie (page 79)
Mid-morning snack	Bowl of oatmeal with cinnamon and fresh berries
Lunch	Super Stacked Veggie "Burgers" (page 104) with side salad
Mid-afternoon snack	Gerrie's Favorite Popcorn Snack (page 114)
Dinner	Your favorite homemade loaded veggie pizza
Dessert	Fudgy Good Frozen Treats (page 152)

Sunday

Breakfast	Gerrie's Favorite Breakfast Skillet (page 79)
Mid-morning snack	Fresh seasonal fruit
Lunch	Super Stacked Veggie "Burgers" (page 104)
Mid-afternoon snack	Raw nuts and/or seeds
Dinner	One Pot Meal Soup (page 98)
Dessert	Fudgy Good Frozen Treats (page 152)

MENU 2

Following the same mantra as above, by cooking just a few of the dishes in this menu, you'll have enough to use throughout the week, both in their original form and within other meals.

Monday

Breakfast	Loaded Oatmeal (page 76) (Save leftovers for Tuesday.)
Mid-morning snack	Veggie sticks or pita with hummus
Lunch	Sandwich with Kenter Canyon Greens Goddess Dressing (page 140) lettuce, tomato, and Sweet and Smoky Tempeh Strips (page 87) (Save leftovers.)
Mid-afternoon snack	Dried fruits and nuts
Dinner	Tahini Noodle Bowl (page 136) (Save leftovers.)
Dessert	Tropical Fruit Cobbler (page 148) (Save leftovers for Tuesday.)

Tuesday

Breakfast	Leftover Loaded Oatmeal
Mid-morning snack	Veggie sticks or pita with hummus
Lunch	Make a Salad a Meal (page 100) with leftover Kenter Canyon Greens Goddess Dressing or leftover sauce from the Tahini Noodle Bowl; add leftover Sweet and Smoky Tempeh Strips for extra flavor and protein.
Mid-afternoon snack	Veggie sticks or pita with hummus
Dinner	New England-Can-Kiss-My-Clam Chowder (page 92) and a side salad using the leftover Kenter Canyon Green Goddess Dressing or leftover sauce from the Tahini Noodle Bowl. If you want to get fancy, you can make homemade bread bowls using the bread bowl variation of the Pizza Dough recipe (page 136).
Dessert	Leftover Tropical Fruit Cobbler

Wednesday

Breakfast	Walnut Chorizo Breakfast Bowl (page 88) (Save leftovers.)
Mid-morning snack	Veggie sticks or pita with hummus
Lunch	Tu-Not Salad (page 112) on a sandwich with leftover Sweet and Smoky Tempeh Strips, lettuce, tomato, and avocado
Mid-afternoon snack	Fresh fruit
Dinner	Make a Salad a Meal (page 100) with leftover Kenter Canyon Greens Goddess Dressing or leftover sauce from the Tahini Noodle Bowl. You can also add a scoop of the Tu-Not salad for extra flavor.
Dessert	Pineapple, Mango, Coconut, and Chia Seed Pudding (page 157) (Save leftovers.)

Thursday

Breakfast	Leftover Walnut Chorizo Breakfast Bowl wrapped in a burrito with avocado
Mid-morning snack	Dried fruit and nuts
Lunch	Brown rice with veggies and leftover Sweet and Smoky Tempeh Strips, topped with leftover sauce from the Tahini Noodle Bowl
Mid-afternoon snack	Incredibly Delicious Kale Chips (page 120) (Save leftovers.)
Dinner	Leftover Clam Chowder and a Tu-Not Salad Melt, on two slices of whole wheat bread and a schmear of Cashew "Cheesy" Sauce (page 142) or two slices of your favorite vegan cheese
Dessert	Leftover Pineapple, Mango, Coconut, and Chia Seed Pudding

Friday

Breakfast	Leftover Walnut Chorizo Breakfast Bowl wrapped into a burrito with avocado
Mid-morning snack	Fresh fruit
Lunch	Make a Salad a Meal (page 100) with leftover Kenter Canyon Greens Goddess Dressing or leftover sauce from the Tahini Noodle Bowl. You can also add a scoop of the Tu-Not salad for extra flavor.
Mid-afternoon snack	Incredibly Delicious Kale Chips (page 120)
Dinner	Garbage Pizza! (Make up a batch of Pizza Dough (page 136) and top it with all the yummy leftovers in the fridge! Save the leftovers for Saturday.)
Dessert	Leftover Pineapple, Mango, Coconut, and Chia Seed Pudding

Saturday

Breakfast	Down-Home Country Tofu Scramble (page 75)
Mid-morning snack	Dried fruits and nuts
Lunch	Leftover Garbage Pizza
Mid-afternoon snack	Leftover Pineapple, Mango, Coconut, and Chia Seed Pudding
Dinner	Italian "Sausage" (page 124) with grilled onions and peppers as a sandwich and "No One Will Know It's Vegan" Potato Salad (page 103) (Save leftovers of both for Sunday.)
Dessert	Tropical Fruit Cobbler (page 148)

Sunday

Breakfast	Nutty Fruitcake Pancakes (page 84)
Mid-morning snack	Fresh fruit
Lunch	Leftover Italian "Sausages" and "No One Will Know It's Vegan" Potato Salad
Mid-afternoon snack	Dried fruits and nuts
Dinner	Roasted Sweet Potato and Sage Raviolis (page 129)
Dessert	Leftover Tropical Fruit Cobbler with Cashew Cream (page 144)

Weekly WellBeing Shopping List

Copy and laminate this shopping list so you can use it over and over again.

Vinegars

- ☐ Apple cider vinegar
- ☐ Balsamic vinegar
- ☐ Brown rice vinegar
- ☐ Red wine vinegar
- ☐ Rice wine vinegar

Spices/Herbs

- ☐ Allspice
- ☐ Basil
- ☐ Blended spices
- ☐ Cayenne pepper
- ☐ Chili powder
- ☐ Chipotle powder
- ☐ Cilantro
- ☐ Cloves
- ☐ Cinnamon
- ☐ Cumin
- ☐ Garlic, fresh
- ☐ Garlic, powder
- ☐ Green onion
- ☐ Nutmeg
- ☐ Onion powder
- ☐ Oregano
- ☐ Pepper
- ☐ Red pepper flakes
- ☐ Rosemary
- ☐ Sage
- ☐ Thyme
- ☐ Turmeric
- ☐ Vanilla

Flours

- ☐ Coconut
- ☐ Cornmeal
- ☐ Oat
- ☐ Quinoa
- ☐ Spelt
- ☐ Whole wheat
- ☐ Whole wheat pastry

Bread/Pasta

- ☐ Corn tortillas
- ☐ Sprouted grain
- ☐ Sprouted tortillas
- ☐ Whole wheat pasta

Whole Grains

- ☐ Amaranth
- ☐ Barley
- ☐ Basmati
- ☐ Brown rice
- ☐ Corn
- ☐ Kamut
- ☐ Millet
- ☐ Oats/oatmeal
- ☐ Quinoa
- ☐ Spelt
- ☐ Wheat berries
- ☐ Wild rice

Dry Beans

- ☐ Bean mix
- ☐ Black
- ☐ Blackeye
- ☐ Canned beans
- ☐ Garbanzo
- ☐ Kidney
- ☐ Lentils
- ☐ Lima
- ☐ Navy

Beverages

- ☐ Coffee
- ☐ Juice
- ☐ Nut/seed milk
- ☐ Tea
- ☐ Water

Frozen Items

- ☐ Brown rice
- ☐ Corn
- ☐ Fruits
- ☐ Greens
- ☐ Peas

Proteins

- ☐ Organic textured vegetable protein (TVP)
- ☐ Seitan
- ☐ Tempeh
- ☐ Tofu

Nuts, Seeds, and Nut Butters

Almonds
- ☐ Cashews
- ☐ Coconut
- ☐ Flax
- ☐ Peanuts
- ☐ Pecans
- ☐ Pumpkin
- ☐ Sunflower seeds
- ☐ Walnuts

EXTRAS

- ☐ Baked chips
- ☐ Braggs Liquid Aminos
- ☐ Coconut Aminos
- ☐ Dried fruit
- ☐ Dry active yeast
- ☐ Hummus
- ☐ Lemon juice
- ☐ Low-salt tamari
- ☐ Mustard
- ☐ Miso
- ☐ Nutritional yeast
- ☐ Pasta sauce
- ☐ Seaweed
- ☐ Vegetable broth

Tomatoes

- ☐ Diced
- ☐ Paste
- ☐ Sauce

Seasonal Produce

_____
_____
_____
_____
_____
_____
_____
_____

Additional Items

_____
_____
_____
_____
_____
_____
_____
_____

Chapter 8

Beyond the Plate

WellBeings care about more than just what we eat! WeBes strive for healthy lifestyles.

Our compassion extends beyond the plate. We volunteer at animal shelters, we cook for homeless shelters, and we have vegan bake sales to raise money for charity.

WeBes also care about the other ways in which animal products are used within our lives, and we do our best to avoid them. Cosmetics, body care, household cleaning products, and clothing all have the potential for animal abuse either by using animal ingredients or by testing on animals. Here are some ways to go vegan—beyond the plate.

Buy Certified Vegan

Look for products that are certified vegan or cruelty free by looking for the following designations or symbols on the packaging. Vegan Action (www.vegan.org), The Vegan Society (www.vegansociety.com), People for the Ethical Treatment of Animals (www.peta.org), as well as a handful of others are responsible for certifying hundreds of companies and products as meeting the requirements for being vegan, including ingredients and sub ingredients, as well as verifying that no animals or animal products were used or tested on, in the processing or refining of ingredients.

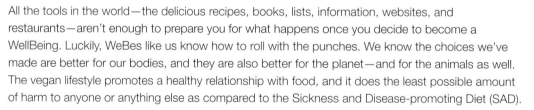

Navigate the Negativity

Now that you've decided to give up all animal products in your diet, you'll start to notice that, all of a sudden, people who couldn't have cared less about what you ate in the past are now suddenly concerned about your dietary choices. Believe it or not, people will be angry with you, whether it's from guilt, jealousy, or an insecurity about their own personal dietary choices. You won't believe the hurtful things people will say to you about your choice to become vegan.

All the tools in the world—the delicious recipes, books, lists, information, websites, and restaurants—aren't enough to prepare you for what happens once you decide to become a WellBeing. Luckily, WeBes like us know how to roll with the punches. We know the choices we've made are better for our bodies, and they are also better for the planet—and for the animals as well. The vegan lifestyle promotes a healthy relationship with food, and it does the least possible amount of harm to anyone or anything else as compared to the Sickness and Disease-promoting Diet (SAD).

Kill 'Em with Kindness

You've heard the saying, "You catch more flies with honey (well, in this case, agave!) than you do with vinegar." It totally applies here. Here are a few tips to help navigate the negativity.

Don't get defensive. Most negative comments come from a place of ignorance. We all have to learn. Instead of getting hurt or defensive, take the opportunity to teach. Or, taking a page from Doug Lisle (author of *The Pleasure Trap* and *Losing Weight without Losing Your Mind*), you don't have to make much of a comment at all. Simply tell people that this is something you are trying, and it seems to be working for you. By doing so, you are not making their choices seem wrong, or making it appear that your choices are better than theirs. It is simply something you are doing because it seems right for you.

Arm yourself with answers. Know the numbers and the facts and reasons why you're doing what you're doing. We've given you many of the answers you will need right in this book. Learn to articulate yourself in a non-threatening, non-accusatory fashion, so when people ask you, "But, where do you get your protein?" you can confidently answer, no matter how badly you want to just roll your eyes!

Don't be preachy: It's hard not to get overly excited when you've found something that improves your life and the well-being of our planet. We know. You've found the best way of living, and you want to shout it from the rooftops and tell everyone. But remember, before you *were* vegan, you *weren't*. To be perfectly honest, unless someone is asking you, no one wants to hear about your personal eating habits. Sometime even when they ask you, they are not ready to hear what you have to say. So go easy and teach by example rather than words as much as possible.

Be a living example. Remember that "Actions speak louder than words." Show the world how easy it is to be vegan. Be a living, shining example of a WellBeing, happy, healthy, and enjoying a plant-based life. By showing everyone else how easy and amazing the lifestyle is, people will want to do what you do.

Resources

Below are websites and resources we use often for products and information, as well as a sense of community. If you live in an area where there isn't a health food store or co-op on every corner, the Internet can be a great source of connection. You can purchase just about anything online these days, and we guarantee there's another WeBe out there in a tiny meat-and-potatoes town just waiting to wax philosophic about the trials and tribulations of being a small-town vegan.

Amazon You can buy just about anything on Amazon, from cookbooks to nutritional yeast. Amazon sells it all, often at prices well below those in brick-and-mortar stores.

Fat Free Vegan Kitchen (fatfreevegan.com) Susan Voisin has become known as the Fat Free Vegan. Even though there are numerous websites full of great recipes on the Internet, Susan's site has a wonderful blog that supplies incredibly delicious recipes that require little to no "reworking" to fit the oil-free, sugar-free way of eating. Check her out!

Food Fight! Grocery (FoodFightGrocery.com) From soap to vegan marshmallows, this all-vegan grocery store has a physical store in Portland, Oregon's, famed vegan mini mall, but you can shop online as well.

Food Not Bombs (FoodNotBombs.net) There are hundreds of autonomous chapters sharing free vegetarian food with hungry people and protesting war and poverty. Food Not Bombs is not a charity. This energetic grassroots movement is active throughout the Americas, Europe, Africa, the Middle East, Asia, and Australia. Food Not Bombs is organizing for peace and an end to the occupations of Iraq, Afghanistan, and Palestine. For more than twenty-five years, the movement has worked to end hunger and has supported actions to stop the globalization of the economy, cease the restrictions to the movements of people, end exploitation, and the destruction of the earth.

Herbivore Clothing (HerbivoreClothing.com) Also located in the vegan mini mall, Herbivore Clothing carries books, t-shirts, hoodies, belts, wallets, and other fun stuff, all carrying a vegan message of compassion.

The Post Punk Kitchen (thePPK.com) Founded by best-selling cookbook author and all-around awesome vegan Isa Chandra Moskowitz, this website is home to her blog and recipes, as well as a very active forum community where vegans of all ages from around the world can gather to chat about parenting and pets to food photography to the latest vegan food trends.

Self Nutrition Data Website (nutritiondata.self.com) This website provides one of the most amazingly complete nutritional breakdowns for different foods. It's a great and very reliable source for becoming more familiar with the nutritional profile of the food you're eating.

Weekly Nutrition Facts (nutritionfacts.org) Michael Greger, M.D., does a beautiful job of combing through all of the hundreds of research papers published weekly and creating a 3- to 5-minute video summarizing the most interesting and relevant papers pertaining to nutrition. None of us has the time, patience, or knowledge to read and understand all of these very technically written papers. You can sign up for Dr. Greger's weekly email at the above site, and it's *free*!

Worldwide Vegan Bake Sale (VeganBakeSale.org) This website has everything you need—including photos, posters, links, and handouts—to help you organize a vegan bake sale for the charity of your choice.

Acknowledgments

This book would not have been possible if it weren't for some amazing people who helped us along the way. As always, the fine folks at Fair Winds Press have helped us to put together an awesome book. From the fonts to the layout of the table of contents, we couldn't have done it without our designers Rita Sowins and Sylvia McArdle. Amanda Waddell, thank you for being a continued inspiration, an amazing person, and for your continued support and faith over the years. Special thanks to Cheryl Winters-Tetreau for helping us to make this book flow. To Heather Godin, Katie Fawkes, Winnie Prentiss, Betsy Gammons, Jennifer Bright-Reich, and the rest of the amazing Fair Winds staff for putting together such a beautiful book. We know that all of you work very hard to make sure that each and every page is laid out and designed with such care and attention to detail. We're so lucky to have you on our team!

To the sweet, loving, compassionate, and talented Celine Steen, you have once again taken our recipes and turned them into mouthwatering pieces of art. Your pictures make this book the beauty that it is, and without them, our recipes would simply be words on a page. Thank you.

To our amazing testers, thank you so much for your hard work, honest feedback, and willingness to try out recipes all for the sake of veganism. You are truly appreciated and loved! We wanted to share some of their advice and experiences here.

Katie Hay: "Being vegan isn't as daunting or scary as it may seem now. It's a journey, with each step more rewarding than the last."

Rochelle Kregar-West, who tweets at @rpkregar: "It's much easier to switch to veganism than you may think. And many people are at different stages on the path. Any change toward it will make you feel better. Don't feel like a failure if you don't make a complete switch in a single day. Do it at the pace that is right for you."

Jessica Eagle, who blogs at cuisinedeseagle.blogspot.ca: "Becoming vegan or a vegan diet can be healthy and have many positive health benefits. However, ensure that it's well planned and nutritionally balanced. Take it one day at a time and trust your inner feeling. Your body knows what is best for you! This book is a wonderful start for your journey!"

Liz Wyman, who blogs at cookingtheveganbooks.com and tweets at @efcliz: "Focus on what you can eat, not what you can't!"

Anna Holt (and sons) who blog at vegfoodforthought. wordpress.com and tweet at @finallywakingup: "Try to think of meals in a new way, the standard omnivore 'something with potatoes and 2 vegetables' is very limiting. Vegan food opens up a wide world of different types of dishes and meals for you to experiment with!"

Sara Rose, who blogs at busyveganmama.blogspot .com: "Baby steps! It doesn't have to be all or nothing, right away. Try new recipes when you can, and stock your pantry as you go."

Karen Lowry: "Educate yourself! Take the time to inform yourself of the benefits of a vegan diet, proper nutrition, and how to handle social situations."

Kelly Klepfer, who blogs at kellyklepfer.blogspot.com: "Going Vegan was a challenge for me as a cook. Cookbooks were invaluable until I got my retaught cooking sea legs. Be patient with yourself."

Jenna Patton and Russell Patton: "Try new ingredients when you find them. Testing for this book made us finally go out and find jackfruit. There are always new things to try!"

Catherine Ballway: "Embrace the [delicious] adventure!"

Jody Weiner, who blogs at vegchic.blogspot.com: "First, going vegan opened my eyes to so many new foods, don't be afraid to branch out. Second, don't focus on whether something tastes like the omni version, does it stand on its own?"

Thom Harr, who blogs at vegantrash.tumblr.com and tweets at @vegantrash: "You will notice that your friends, family, and co-workers will have a harder time understanding your vegan diet than you will. Surround yourself with like-minded individuals, whether it is by joining a vegan meet-up group, reading blogs online, or by frequenting vegan establishments. You are never alone."

Angela Ramsammy, who tweets at @angelaramsammy: "Cheese is like crack; once you kick it, being vegan is easy!"

Doe Mora: "Becoming vegan can seem daunting, but eating raw cookie batter without eggs is priceless! Plus it's fun to actually make the cookies and impress your friends who ask: 'no eggs?'"

Dana Vickerson, who blogs at vanishingveggie.com: "Don't get discouraged if people give you a hard time. They will come around when they see how positive veganism can be in your life."

Daneen Agecoutay, who blogs at thegroovegardenonline.com: "Read as much as you can about veganism. There is power in knowledge."

Kyleigh Rapanos, who blogs at thegoodkarmakitchen.blogspot.com: "Have patience with yourself. If you slip, don't sweat it, don't dwell on it, just keep moving forward and it'll keep getting easier."

Melissa McPherson who posts on instagram @ hopshackchronicles: "Use Internet/Instagram/Twitter/social media to find vegan blogs and awesome people who you can learn recipes from, be inspired by, and become part of the vegan community!"

Mathilde Poulin: "Word of wisdom: Don't go vegan for your friends. Do it for yourself, to have a clear conscience."

Rebecca Bolduc: "Read the many available blogs and don't be afraid to experiment."

Allison Cabel: "Get some cookbooks or find recipes online and get in the kitchen! Share your vegan meals with friends and family."

Maud Pryor, who blogs at feudfood.blogspot.com: "Diving in or dabbling, any step towards veganism is a step in the right direction!"

Karen Ruggero, katanacakes.com: "Eat more veggies!"

Claudia Desmarais: "Veganism is the best gift you can offer your conscience, as well as the world you and other beings share."

Kelly Cavalier: "Be open to trying new cuisines and ingredients. There are so many things I thought I didn't like that I love now!"

Jennifer Tutor: "Being new to veganism, I was very surprised to discover that rather than limiting my eating, it has opened up endless possibilities!"

Courtney Blair: "Don't be scared to try new things. It is an adventure, and you will discover so many new foods and flavors you love!"

Michelle Truty, who blogs at VegtasticVoyage.com and tweets @VegtasticVoyage: "There's no teleporting in veganism. It's a path and you need to walk it, but it's a pretty great path for you, for the world, and for the animals. The breadth of vegan food is so vast. Get excited, try everything (twice), and make it your own."

Dana Grothaus: "When you know better, you do better." —Maya Angelou

Jennifer Hogle, who tweets @ babygotbok: "Find a Vegan BFF and share every new vegan dish you make with each other!"

Kaycee Bassett, who blogs at veganmachine.com

Audrey Singaraju: "Use all of the great resources available, such as cookbooks, blogs, and people to make going vegan easy!"

With thanks from Gerrie: I would like to first and foremost thank God, from Whom I believe all things have been created and all life exists. It was an answer to prayer that brought Joni and I together to co-author this book. I would also like to thank my family who has put up with and continues to put up with me as I tirelessly subject them to my opinions and WellBeing ways. It would not have been possible for me to write this book if it had not been for Whole Foods Market and the position as healthy eating specialist that I have been blessed with over the past four years. If it had not been for this position, I probably would not have had the opportunity to study and learn from such nutritional giants as Dr. Colin Campbell, Dr. Caldwell Esselstyn, Rip Esselstyn, Dr. Joel Fuhrman, and Dr. John McDougall. There are more than 200 years of research and factual information between these incredibly forward-thinking men that proves beyond a doubt that a diet consisting of plants and whole, minimally processed foods prevents and reverses most known diseases. Thank you to Whole Foods Market and John Mackey for truly caring about people's health and helping to spread the research findings of these incredible doctors to the public.

I would also like to thank Tammy Lopes (accomplished plant-based chef and very special friend) whom I have had the pleasure of working with over the past four years. She has taught me the secrets of how to make a plant-based diet amazingly delicious without using fats, sugars, and oils.

And last, I would like to thank my co-author, Joni, for inviting me to write this book with her and for putting up with my inexperience at writing recipe books! Hugs to all!

With thanks from Joni: I would like to personally thank my husband for once again giving up space in the refrigerator, cupboards, and generally letting me take over the whole kitchen—make that the whole house!—as I tinkered and tested out new recipes, never complaining (okay, well sometimes complaining) when I opted to stay home to work on the book instead of going out on a date.

I would also like to thank my sweet friend Jennifer Shrier, who, although not vegan (yet!) has always supported me and inspires me to be myself, take risks, and reminds me to get out and have fun every now and again! I love you, Jennifer.

And, of course, I would like to extend a heartfelt and big fat thanks to my friend Gerrie, who brought her nutritional expertise and passion for healthy eating to this book, and also into my life. She has made this a book about going vegan, and also one that can get you healthy, too! Thanks, Gerrie! Can you believe we did it?

About the Authors

Gerrie Adams

Driven by a passion to help people and demonstrate that whole, unprocessed food is a vital link to health, Gerrie changed her career at midlife. She started her quest to help people reverse diseases and achieve optimum health through a plant-based diet by receiving her B.S. in Food Science with emphasis in Nutrition. She currently works with Whole Foods Market as a Healthy Eating Specialist, where she has had the opportunity to study with and learn from renowned plant-based doctors and nutritional researchers. In addition to working for Whole Foods Market, Gerrie is the founder of the non-profit organization Fostering Hopes and Dreams. This organization donates profits from Gerrie's healthy eating retreats to foster children programs. You can contact Gerrie via email at gerrielynn.adams@yahoo.com.

Joni Marie Newman

Joni currently resides in Southern California with her husband, Dan, sweet evil ground monkey, Annie, and old lady ghostface, Maxine. They share a tiny cottage in one of the last rural parts of Orange County. In this cottage, Joni plots to make the whole world vegan—one vegan taco at a time. Through Joni's cooking, blog, and books, she aims to prove that it's not necessary to murder or torture another living, sentient being to have a tasty supper. She's the founder of JustTheFood.com. You can contact Joni via email at joni@justthefood.com.

Index

Note: <u>Underscored</u> page references indicate boxed text. **Boldface** page references indicate photographs and illustrations.